Cash flow
accounting

The VNR Series in Accounting and Finance

Consulting Editor
John Perrin, Professor and Director of the Centre for Industrial Economic and Business Research, University of Warwick

G.A. Lee
Modern Financial Accounting (3rd edn)

G.A. Lee
Modern Financial Accounting Student's Manual

T.A. Lee
Income and Value Measurement (2nd edn)

T.A. Lee
Company Financial Reporting (2nd edn)

T.A. Lee
Cash Flow Accounting

J.M. Samuels and F.M. Wilkes
The Management of Company Finance (3rd edn)

S.P. Lumby
Investment Appraisal and Related Decisions (2nd edn)

Cash flow accounting

TOM LEE
Professor of Accountancy and Finance, University of Edinburgh
Director of Accounting and Auditing Research, Institute of Chartered Accountants of Scotland

Van Nostrand Reinhold (UK) Co. Ltd

First published in 1984 by
Van Nostrand Reinhold (UK) Co. Ltd
Molly Millars Lane, Wokingham, Berkshire, England

Typeset in 10 on 11pt Sabon by Columns Ltd, Reading

Printed and bound in Great Britain by
The Thetford Press, Norfolk

Library of Congress Cataloging in Publication Data

Lee, Thomas Alexander.
Cash flow accounting.

(The VNR series in accounting and finance)
Bibliography: p.
Includes index.
1. Cash flow—Accounting. I. Title. II. Series.
HF5681.C28L43 1984 657'.48 84-7511
ISBN 0-442-30609-1
ISBN 0-442-30610-5 (pbk.)

Contents

Preface

For many years I have been concerned to challenge the conventional wisdoms of financial accounting, and have been arguing for a system of financial reporting based on the notion of cash flows. I have written many papers on the subject (see the bibliography to this text), and have now reached the stage when I feel it is necessary for me to draw them together into a coherent whole in which my approach to cash flow reporting is decribed and explained. My previous papers tend to reflect my thoughts on relevant topics at particular points in time, but, as these thoughts have tended to change and develop over time, it appeared that a text would be a suitable way of putting forward an up-to-date account of my approach to cash flow reporting.

As the previous paragraph has indicated this text is concerned with the subject-matter of accounting for, and disclosing, cash flow-based information within the context of external financial reporting. As such, it deals with the reporting of realized cash flows and potential cash flows in the form of sale prices. My thoughts on cash flow reporting have developed to the stage at which I believe the latter can only be achieved meaningfully if sale price-based accounting is involved in addition to the more straightforward practices of accounting for actual cash flows. As such, my recommended system of cash flow reporting will depend as much on the ideas of so-called exit value theorists (such as R.J. Chambers and R.R. Sterling) as it does on the ideas of the pure cash flow reporting proponents (such as G.H. Lawson and myself).

When planning the text, I was faced with several serious problems. First, was it to be a rigorous analysis of the ideas of all cash flow reporting advocates (including, possibly, G.H. Lawson, B. Hicks, A.L. Thomas and L.C. Heath) or should it be limited to the approach that I advocate personally? I decided on the latter course of action as I felt that cash flow reporting was in its relative infancy – the relevant literature being full of undeveloped ideas with few attempts at describing what could be termed a full system of reporting. I therefore thought that, if I could specify a model of reporting, even if only in my own terms, this could be used as a basis for further development and discussion. I hope that this has provided a focus for both supporters and critics of cash flow reporting, in a way that a more neutral and broader approach would have failed to do. Readers will therefore find that, although other writers are referred to when relevant, the major sources for ideas for this text stems from my earlier writings. I have done this as a matter of deliberate policy, but in no way as a discourtesy to other writers on cash flow accounting.

Second, I found it difficult to decide on an approach and style to adopt for the text. I believe it will be used mainly in more advanced courses in financial accounting because of the detailed attention that is paid in introductory and intermediate courses to conventional systems of reporting based on historic costs and, possibly, current costs. However, the ideas contained in this text are exceedingly fundamental. Indeed, in an ideal world, I believe they ought to be introduced at the introductory level. But the real world intrudes on these notions, and I was therefore faced with the question of how to present relatively uncomplicated material to relatively advanced student readers in a way that best suited their state of knowledge.

I decided that even advanced students of accounting can lack confidence in accounting practices owing to the limitations of the classroom. Many years of teaching experience have caused me to appreciate that you can never make ideas simple enough for them. I therefore adopted an approach to the content of the text that was to make it as simple as possible – particularly in the opening chapters where conventional ideas are challenged. In order to reinforce the argument, I adopted a style that makes continuous use of simple numerical examples, and I make no apologies for their profusion. The book is a teaching text which should be used over a period of time. The ideas are severe challenges to the conventional ideas of financial reporting theory and practice. Students must be given as much help as possible in this process. Otherwise, the teaching of financial reporting becomes an exercise reminiscent of Pavlov – conventional wisdom one day; unconventional challenge the next day.

The simple exercises are therefore provided for the student as a toe-hold to confirm what is being stated verbally. Of course many of the examples may appear very simple to an advanced student or teacher of accounting. But when the orthodox is being challenged, nothing can be regarded as simple. In any case, there is no guarantee that the reader will have a relatively advanced knowledge of accounting. The text may be used on postgraduate business courses where the level of accounting knowledge may not be high. Despite assuming a prior knowledge, the text does make allowances for those readers with only an introductory knowledge.

So far as I am aware, no other text exists that attempts to draw together the ideas of cash flow accounting and exit value accounting in a unified system of reporting that is explained in simple terms. The text is not a research monograph and should be regarded as a teaching book. It is an attempt to identify the type of financial reporting that is relevant to the needs of various report users who appear to be concerned with matters relating to entity liquidity and profitability. The present rather sterile debate concerning reporting alternatives to historic costs has become confused and confusing because more attention is paid to the problems of financial reporters and auditors than to the needs of report users. This text attempts to redress this imbalance, and to provide a content that is relevant to the current interest in entity cash flows.

And now a few words of warning to the reader – in the first place relating to specific terminology used in the text. Part of the difficulty associated with the literature of financial reporting is that the nature of the concept of profit is confused. Although it is a man-made construct with no tangible form, it is often attributed with a tangible meaning particularly when it is used within the context of decisions such as those concerned with distribution. Because I believe it could bring chaos to the text to break away completely from conventional descriptions of these matters, I decided to use these descriptions – for example, 'profit available for distribution'. In fact the text will argue that it is cash that is usually distributed and not profit, which should be regarded only as an indicator of the availability of such cash. Thus, the reader is warned that statements in the text such as 'profit available for distribution or retention' are made solely in the context of profit being used as an indicator of cash available for distribution. As the text will reveal, it can be an exceedingly poor indicator.

The other major terminology problem in the text is concerned with the concept of realization. Conventionally, this is interpreted in terms of cash or near-cash transactions, and means that credit purchases and sales are regarded as realizations. For purposes of cash flow accounting and reporting, I take a much narrower view of realization – that is, strictly in terms of cash. Thus, items such as debtors and creditors are treated as 'unrealized' within the text. Although I recognize the alternative approach, I feel that cash flow reporting should relate as much as possible to the flow of cash – there is no guarantee that debtors will be received in full and creditors will be settled at the amount stated.

On a further matter of caution, I think it is important to state at the outset that this text is concerned with financial reporting of an ex post nature. This is not to deny the potential utility of such matters as forecast statements. Indeed, in most of my prior writings on cash flow accounting, I have argued for the inclusion of cash flow forecasts and related information. However, the issue of reporting forecasts is a vexed one which contains many unresolved matters, and I am anxious to place my ideas on cash flow reporting within a feasible context. Therefore I have taken the approach of explaining my ideas on cash flow within a conventional framework of management reporting on its past actions to a variety of external interests.

The final caveat to the reader is in the form of advice. The text has been constructed deliberately as a series of related chapters. Thus, I hope the reader will not be tempted to avoid certain chapters merely because they are familiar and do not appear to add to his or her knowledge. This is particularly the case with Chapters 3 and 4 where the traditional approach to financial reporting is examined – that is, the measurements of periodic income and related capital through the use of valuation and capital maintenance procedures. Much of the discussion in these chapters is designed to examine these traditions as they are applied in a variety of income models (some already in practice, and some not), and as a means of helping to justify the use of a non-traditional reporting of related cash flows in which income and capital notions are not central features.

From the above comments, it should be clear to the reader that this text is very much a personal approach to cash flow accounting and reporting. It is not intended as the definitive version because the subject is insufficiently developed for that to be the case. However, it is at a point in its development when an argument and explanation can take place. This is the purpose of this text, and the first chapter sets the scene by questioning the meaning of the traditional measurements of income, financial position and funds flow which are reported today.

TOM LEE
Edinburgh

NOTE

Throughout the text there is a constant use of quantitative examples for illustrative purposes. In order to allow the reader to check the computation and derivation of individual figures, workings have been provided at the end of the book. It is hoped that student readers particularly will use these workings as answers with which to check their calculations.

CHAPTER 1 Profit, cash and financial position

INTRODUCTION

Consider the following financial situation:

AB purchases one unit of stock on credit for £70. He then sells it on credit for £100. Assuming no other transactions, and a tax rate of 50% of realized profit, the undernoted outline financial statements can be produced to describe these activities:

PROFIT STATEMENT

	£
Sale	100
Less: cost of sale	70
Profit before tax	30
Less: tax provision	15
Profit after tax	15

The realized profit before tax on these transactions is therefore £30, and the realized profit after tax and available for distribution is £15.

BALANCE SHEET

	£	£
Debtor		100
Less: creditor	70	
taxation	15	85
Profit retained		15

Thus, AB appears to be 'better off' by £15 following these transactions, and may regard this figure as being 'consumable' in the form of a distribution.

FUNDS STATEMENT

	£
Source of funds	
Profit before tax	30
Application of funds	
Increase in debtor	100
Less: increase in creditor	70
Increase in working capital	30

The funds statement reveals that the realized profit before tax was used to fund an equivalent increase of working capital.[1]*

In summary, therefore, a realized profit of £30 has been achieved, of which £15 is required to cover a tax provision; leaving the remainder as the periodic increase in AB's capital, and available for distribution. The £30 of profit before tax has been utilized to aid the funding of a £30 increase in working capital. It is a situation that conforms with conventional accounting practice based on the principles of historic cost, realization and matching.

However, there is a further means of assessing these figures. In particular, it is important to recognise that there have been no accompanying cash transactions, and the consequence of this is that there has been no equivalent realization of cash to follow the earning of the realized profit of £30. In other words, the realization of a profit of £30 has not meant there has been an equivalent inflow of cash of £30.

The constraints of this situation are reasonably clear. The profit after tax of £15 could be distributed legitimately, leaving AB apparently no worse off in monetary terms than he was at the time immediately preceding these transactions. But AB has no cash and would require to borrow £15 in order to do this. He may convince his bank manager that he is doing so on the basis of increasing his working capital. If a cash distribution of £15 was then made, and borrowings of an equivalent amount were obtained, AB's balance sheet position would be as follows:

BALANCE SHEET

	£	£
Debtor		100
Less: creditor	70	
bank	15	
taxation	15	100
Profit retained		—

He would therefore appear to be no worse off financially than he was before the stock transactions, and would have enjoyed the consumption of his dividend of £15.

* Notes and references appear on page 134.

But much depends on the recoverability of the £100 debtor. The 'best' financial position AB can be in is to recover the £100, pay his creditor £70 and the tax authority £15, leaving £15 to repay his bank borrowing. The 'worst' possible situation would be one involving the irrecoverability of the debtor, leaving AB's balance sheet as follows:

BALANCE SHEET

	£	£
Debtor		—
Less: creditor	70	
taxation	—	
bank	15	85
Profit retained		(85)

Owing to the trading loss caused by the bad debt, no tax provision would be necessary. But AB would be £85 worse off because of these further transactions, and there would obviously be no funds available for any repayment of the creditor or the bank.

PROFITABILITY AND LIQUIDITY

What this arguably over-simplified example is attempting to clarify is that conventional accounting practice may not provide sufficient information regarding the underlying liquidity position of the entity. Conventional practice, even if based on the apparently conservative principle of realization, can be potentially misleading if not adapted to provide information on both profitability and liquidity. This can be more clearly seen in a further example of a more complex nature.

CD commences business with £80 of capital represented by an equivalent bank balance. During his first period of trading, he enters into the following summarized transactions:

Item traded	*1* £	*2* £	*3* £	*4* £	*5* £	*6* £	*Total* £
Purchased on credit	20	20	25	25	30	30	150
Amount paid	20	20	25	25	—	—	90
Sold on credit	28	28	28	36	—	—	120
Amount received	28	28	—	—	—	—	56

Assuming a 'first-in, first-out' basis of stock accounting, and a 50% tax rate based on realized profit, CD's financial statements for this period would be:

PROFIT STATEMENT

	£
Sales (a)*	120
Less: cost of sales (b)	90
Profit before tax	30
Less: tax provision	15
Profit after tax	15

This statement reveals a realized profit on the first four items sold of £30, one half of which requires to be set aside to cover tax due at 50% of profit. The remaining £15 would be available for distribution.

BALANCE SHEET

	£	£
Stock (c)		60
Debtors (d)		64
Bank (e)		46
		170
Less: creditors (f)	60	
taxation	15	75
		95
Capital		80
Profit retained		15
		95

CD has improved his capital position by £15 over the period; he has a comfortable net working capital base; and he has liquid and near-liquid assets. He therefore appears to be more than able to make a distribution from the profit retained of £15.

FUNDS STATEMENT

	£
Source of funds	
Profit before tax	30
Application of funds	
Increase in stock	60
Increase in debtors	64
	124
Less: increase in creditors	60
Increase in working capital	64
Decrease in bank balance (g)	(34)

* Lower case letters indicate that the item is explained in the 'workings' on page 142.

Thus, by generating a realized profit before tax of £30, and utilizing available cash assets of £34, CD has increased his working capital by £64. But a question is raised as to whether or not this information package of allocation and accrual-based financial statements is sufficient to reveal a reasonably complete picture of CD's trading activities.

Despite the fact that the business is liquid at the end of the period, and has generated a realized pre-tax profit of £30, the cash flow of the entity has not been positive. This can be seen by taking the cash figures achieved and suitably matching them:

CASH FLOW STATEMENT

	£
Sales receipts (h)	56
Less: cash payments (i)	90
Operating deficit	(34)

In other words, the fall in the bank balance from £80 to £46 over the period has been due to a trading or operating cash deficit of £34 – two items only being sold and cash recovered, with four items purchased and paid for. The realized profit before tax of £30 has not therefore been recovered totally in cash; instead, there has been a net outflow due to payments exceeding receipts. The difference of £64 between the two figures is due to an increase of working capital of the same amount during the period (stock £60 plus debtors £64 minus creditors £60).

This further example, based on simple figures, has been used to evidence the limitations of traditional accounting practice in its attempt at revealing a picture of trading activity generally and profitability particularly. It is a well known principle of accounting that profit does not necessarily equal cash; and, likewise, it must be further emphasized that realized profit does not necessarily equate with cash flow. Thus, the completeness of an entity's report on its financial activities can be achieved only by providing information on both profitability and liquidity as well as financial position. The funds statement goes some way to meeting this objective but it is not a complete report on entity liquidity.

The problem of the incompleteness of profit-orientated reporting packages is a universal one – that is, it affects all reporting entities (from the largest to the smallest); all report users (owners, lenders, bankers, suppliers, customers, employees, etc.); and is international (and not just a local issue). It would thus appear to be central to any description, explanation and assessment of financial accounting thought. The latter cannot be examined without the limitations of the profit-orientated system being pinpointed.

TEXT OUTLINE

The aim of this text is therefore to explore ways in which the underlying liquidity of a reporting entity can be revealed in accounting terms. As such, it is a book on a cash flow-based accounting theory and practice, and examines these matters in detail. It should not be taken as an attack or a rejection of conventional accounting and reporting of profitability and financial position. The latter have had and will continue to have a considerable part to play in external financial reporting and analysis. But, equally, the need to report on cash flows should be recognised in order to complete the package of relevant financial information. To omit cash flow from the latter creates the attendant risk of report users being ill-informed and/or misled. The consequences of this regarding the rationality of their decisions should be reasonably obvious.

The remainder of the text will be divided between eight further chapters. Chapter 2 deals with the fundamentals of external financial reporting – that is, the need for useful and relevant financial information concerning specified entities; how the present-day system is centred on the measurement and reporting of periodic income; and how the utility and relevance of such a system is increasingly being challenged. The chapter will therefore provide the foundation with which to judge cash flow accounting.

Chapter 3 examines the traditional system of reporting in terms of historic costs, and particularly analyses the meaning of such information. It also explores the nature and meaning of two of the main alternatives to that of historic cost – that is, replacement cost and sale price. The flexibility of allocation, valuation and capital maintenance procedures are introduced.

Chapter 4 questions the accounting and reporting systems outlined in Chapter 3 in relation to the fundamentals specified in Chapter 2 – in particular, utility and relevance, correspondence and comprehensibility.

Chapters 5 and 6 are concerned largely with outlining a total cash flow accounting system that includes both cash flows and sale prices in combinations that appear to meet the information needs of various report user groups, and comply with the fundamental accounting criteria explained in Chapter 2. They are provided as an answer to the criticisms of conventional accounting outlined in Chapters 3 and 4. Chapter 5 specifies the system in detail using a worked example, and Chapter 6 deals specifically with the supporting arguments for a total cash flow accounting system.

The measurement and reporting of cash flows will have been the major subject for Chapters 2 to 6, inclusive. The analysis and interpretation of reported cash flow information are explored in Chapter 7. This involves the suggestion of multi-period aggregations. The analysis is mainly of actual cash flow data, but attention is also paid in Chapter 8 to examining and interpreting potential cash flows as described in terms of changing sale prices. Chapter 9 concludes the text by examining the main difficulties associated with the use of cash flow-based financial information.

SOURCES OF MATERIAL

Much of the work for this book has been published in papers that are listed in the Bibliography. In this sense, the text is a bringing together of ideas developed over several years. It is felt that it is time that they were put together into a coherent whole. The approach will be to provide a reasonably straightforward account of the reasons for and structure of cash flow accounting within the context of external financial reporting. It will assume a knowledge and understanding of conventional accounting theory and practice, and will utilize quantified illustrations wherever relevant and convenient.

CHAPTER 2 Fundamentals of accounting

NATURE OF ACCOUNTING

At its simplest, the role of accounting can be described as the provision of information that is largely of a financial nature. Such a definition, however, is characterized by vagueness, particularly with regard to the nature of the information communicated, the persons to whom it is transmitted, and the uses to which it is put. Thus, a more expansive statement of the role of accounting portrays it as a function in which economic events and activities of a defined entity are measured in mainly monetary terms, and transmitted in suitable information form to persons entitled to receive such information, and who require it for purposes of their specific relationships with the stated entity.

From this statement, it is possible to derive certain key fundamentals of external accounting and reporting that can be used as the foundation for developing the arguments put forward in this text. Such fundamentals include the propositions outlined in the following sections.[2]

INFORMATION AND COMMUNICATION

Accounting is an information/communication function – its purpose is therefore to transmit measured information that is intended to increase the knowledge of its recipient and reduce his uncertainty about the future. Accounting information must have the potential to do these things – that is, it must have utility. This does not mean that it will be of use in every case; only that it is capable of being put to use. If it does not have this potential, it cannot be described as information. It remains as mere data. For example:

EF purchases 6 units of stock for £50 each, and sells 3 units for £75 each. Because he was involved personally in the purchasing and selling of the stock, and has the documentation to evidence this, he has available certain data that do not increase his knowledge. However, they have the potential to be useful if put in a form that provides EF with information capable of satisfying his need for additional knowledge. In this case, when the data are suitably matched, he can be informed about the profitability of such trading, and his knowledge on this matter can thereby be increased. That is:

PROFIT STATEMENT

	£
Sales (a)	225
Less: cost of sales (b)	150
Profit on 3 units	75

Thus, from unorganized accounting data, and by an appropriate application of measurement principles, EF's knowledge of his trading activities can be improved, and he can feed this into whatever decisions he may feel he has to take – for instance, he may have to make a pricing decision concerning the 3 units of unsold stock (for example, whether or not to maintain the current price of £75 per unit). The information therefore has the potential to be applied to such decisions, and satisfies the most fundamental objective of accounting – it should be capable of being used by its recipient to satisfy his need for knowledge of a specified kind (in this case, trading profitability).

RELEVANCE

Accounting information must be relevant to be useful – that is, it should be capable of influencing the behaviour and actions of its recipient. As indicated above, this means in particular that such information must be capable of influencing the decisions of the latter person. It must have the potential to reduce any uncertainty associated with a particular decision by aiding the decision maker to increase his knowledge of the alternatives available, and helping him to interpret the major factors impinging on the decision. For example:

Assume the previous data related to EF, and that his decision concerns the provision of adequate funding to meet his operating commitments. Also assume that he has paid for all his purchases but only received cash for 2 of the units sold. If he received the profit statement describing the realized profit of £75 on 3 units sold, this information could be said to be useful (in a general sense) but not relevant (in a more specific sense). Knowing about the profit of £75 has little direct bearing on a decision concerned with liquidity funding, for what is of relevance in this context is a report on the underlying cash flow from the stated transactions:

CASH FLOW STATEMENT

	£
Sales (c)	150
Less: payment (d)	300
Cash deficit	(150)

From this statement, EF has been informed that an operating cash deficit of

£150 has arisen from lack of cash coming in from customers when considerably greater payments were being made to suppliers. This information, when fed into his funding decision, could be claimed to be both useful and relevant. The profit information, in this case, cannot be said to be relevant until it is brought to bear upon a decision concerning an assessment of profitability. Knowledge of a profit of £75 is misleading in the consideration of a cash deficit of £150.

REPORT USERS

The producer of accounting information should have knowledge of the potential users of such information in order to ensure it is relevant to their needs. The related ideas of information utility and relevance beg the immediate questions of 'useful to whom?' and 'useful for what purpose?'. In other words, accountants cannot afford to be ignorant of the potential needs of the recipients of their information, or they will be reporting 'in the dark' with little idea of the degree of utility and relevance achieved by their communications. This does not mean that they should have a specific need or use in mind – merely a general understanding and knowledge of potential user groups. Thus the information ought to be generally relevant – that is, it should be capable of influencing the decisions of a particular user group without any predetermination of a specific decision.

For example, in the case of EF illustrated above, the accountant concerned could be asked to prepare information for EF's banker – that is, the latter person would be involved in decisions regarding the funding of EF's business, and would require information suitable for this purpose. In these circumstances, knowledge of the general nature of a banker's decisions would be important to the accountant. In this way, he could transmit to the individual banker concerned information regarding the realized profit of £75 and the cash flow deficit of £150. This would enable the banker to select that information which he regarded as specifically relevant to the type of decision he has to make – be that to initiate, continue, expand, reduce or terminate borrowing facilities. With the user selecting information for purposes of his decision, the generally relevant information becomes specifically relevant. But this latter condition is achieved by the user and not by the producer of the information. Thus, the neutrality of the information is preserved – it is not biased to the benefit or detriment of particular users until they make specific use of it.

CORRESPONDENCE[3]

Accounting requires that there be an adequate identification of the economic activities and events of the specified entity that is the subject of such a function. Activity concerning the acquisition, utilization and disposal of scarce economic resources is the main subject of accounting, and it is essential that this is identified properly within an entity structure such that there can be a suitable correspondence between the economic activity being described and the information describing it.

A major problem in this respect is that accounting information is being produced as a surrogate for a direct experience or contact with the economic activity about which knowledge is desired. It is therefore important that the surrogate corresponds with what would have been gained from direct experience. Identification of the activity and the entity within which it takes place is a fundamental part of accounting. For example:

GH buys 10 units of stock item 1 at £9 each. He also buys 16 units of stock item 2 at £11 each. He sells 4 units of 1 at £12 each, and 7 units of 2 at £14 each. He wishes to know the profit he has realized on stock item 2. All transactions are for cash.

What he does not want in this case is either knowledge of the profit realized on stock item 1 – that is:

PROFIT STATEMENT

	£
Sales (e)	48
Less: cost of sales (f)	36
Profit	12

or knowledge of the profit realized on all stock items – that is:

PROFIT STATEMENT

	£
Sales (g)	146
Less: cost of sales (h)	113
Profit	33

or the cash flow from total operations:

CASH FLOW STATEMENT

	£
Sales (i)	146
Less: payments (j)	266
Cash deficit	(120)

For none of these statements would correspond with the activities of which he has no knowledge – that is, realized profits on stock item 2:

PROFIT STATEMENT

	£
Sales (k)	98
Less: cost of sales (l)	77
Profit	21

This last statement corresponds to the economic activity that has been identified as generally relevant to GH. It does not relate to any specific decision, and thus remains neutral. It further emphasizes, however, the need for the accountant to identify the user or user group to which the information is to be directed, and the general need that gives rise to the requirement for it.

MEASUREMENT AND COMMUNICATION

Accounting information requires to be measured and communicated adequately. The correspondence of the information to the economic reality it purports to describe does not just involve an identification of economic activities and events. It also means that the accounting data are measured according to generally acceptable rules that do not distort the surrogate approach to direct experience. For example:

Assume IJ sells insurance policies on a commission basis. His profit for the current period on a cash basis is £5,000 (no allowance being made for the depreciation of his car). The latter asset cost £6,000 at the beginning of the period, and has an estimated useful life of six periods with a negligible and scrap price. Its second-hand price at the end of the current period is £3,500.

It is a generally accepted rule of accounting that some deduction be made for depreciation when determining profit. Thus, it could be argued that IJ's profit for the current period is:

PROFIT STATEMENT

	£
Trading profit	5,000
Less: depreciation (m)	1,000
Profit	4,000

But the question is whether the depreciation provision aids the correspondence of profit with the economic reality underlying it. The above depreciation practice does not contravene generally accepted accounting at the present time. But doubts must exist as to whether or not it reasonably describes the economic reality of either the fall in the sale price of the car:

PROFIT STATEMENT

	£
Trading profit	5,000
Less: fall in sale price of car (n)	2,500
Profit	2,500

or the cash flow of:

CASH FLOW STATEMENT

	£
Trading surplus	5,000
Less: purchase payment for car	6,000
Cash deficit	(1,000)

Arguments can be made that either of the latter two statements corresponds better with the underlying economic reality of the acquisition and holding of the car than does the generally accepted practice, which represents an arithmetical allocation of a past cost datum over the vehicle's useful life. Whatever the approach, it is essential that the method of measurement adopted does not distort the underlying reality being reported. Otherwise correspondence will be achieved inadequately, and the report user can be ill-informed or misled by what he receives.

Proper disclosure and presentation of accounting information is also essential – that is, if the accounting messages that have been measured are to be communicated adequately to their recipients. Poor communication can result in distortions to the detriment of the latter persons, and this reduces the value of the accounting function. This also means that there has to be a communication of the required accounting information in a form that is comprehensible to the report user. If the latter person does not understand, or misunderstands, the accounting messages being transmitted to him, then there is a danger that use of these messages could be damaging financially to him. For example:

Suppose KL has received the following outline financial statements relating to the financial results for his first trading period (assuming his opening position to have been capital of £1,000 represented by a bank balance of that amount).

PROFIT STATEMENT

	£	£
Sales		16,000
Less: cost of sales	15,000	
depreciation of plant	100	15,100
Profit		900

BALANCE SHEET

	£	£	£
Plant (less depreciation)			400
Stock		2,000	
Debtors		2,000	
		4,000	
Less: creditors	1,200		
bank overdraft	1,300	2,500	1,500
			1,900
Capital			1,000
Retained profit			900
			1,900

From these statements, KL can infer that he is £900 'better off' than he was when he commenced the period, and that his net worth has increased by the same amount owing to the profit earned and realized.

Although the statements have been produced using the traditional practices of historic cost accounting, there is a danger that KL (and any other user of the financial statements) may not understand that the profit of £900 has no equivalent cash surplus, and that the total worth of the business (if defined in sale price terms) may not be £1,900. In fact, the cash flow of the business was as follows:

CASH FLOW STATEMENT

	£
Sales	14,000
Less: operating payments	15,800
Trading deficit	(1,800)
Less: payment for plant	500
Total deficit	(2,300)
Add: opening bank balance	1,000
Closing bank overdraft	(1,300)

In other words, although the realized historic cost profit before depreciation was £1,000°, the cash flow equivalent was a deficit of £1,800. In addition, £500 was spent on plant but only £100 was treated as an expense of the period in the form of depreciation. These differences are difficult enough for accountants to comprehend fully, but are considerably more of a problem when non-accounting users are faced with interpreting the data.

As previously mentioned, the comprehension issue may not be confined to periodic trading results. Suppose KL's plant was unsaleable (which would not be unusual) and his stock had a sale price of 70% of its cost of £2,000.

Under these circumstances, and assuming his debtors will pay in full, KL's financial position could be described in sale price terms as:

BALANCE SHEET

	£	£	£
Plant			—
Stock (p)		1,400	
Debtors		2,000	
		3,400	
Less: creditors	1,200		
bank overdraft	1,300	2,500	900
			900
Capital			1,000
Profit retained		900	
Less: fall in value of:			
plant (q)	400		
stock (r)	600	1,000	(100)
			900

Far from having a business worth £1,900, and being £900 'better off' than when he commenced, KL appears to be worth £900 and is £100 less 'well-off'. The point here is not so much the appropriateness of the figures – the historic cost set is based on one group of accounting principles and the sale price equivalent is based on an alternative group. The basic issue is the difficulty caused by KL receiving one set using certain principles and possibly believing that they represent another set using other principles. Such confusion is a distinct possibility – and a dangerous one if decisions are taken on the basis of such a misunderstanding.[4] Thus, the user must receive information that he understands fully and, because it is intended to correspond to an economic reality which he cannot experience directly, it should provide him with an undistorted view of that reality. He is entitled to assume lack of distortion – accounting should not be a service to which the principle of caveat emptor applies.

This last point brings the discussion on comprehension to the producer of the communicated information. The latter material must be prepared and disclosed in such a way as not to distort the economic reality that is being described as a surrogate experience for the user. If it is distorted then, no matter how good the user's powers of comprehension, he could be misled through his use of the information for purposes of his decisions. For example:

The financial statements of MN for the most recent period of his trading have been drawn up on the basis of historic cost accounting. The accountant involved in their preparation has treated major repairs and maintenance on plant of £2,500 as an addition to plant. One tenth of this cost has been written off as depreciation during the period. The completed statements are as follows:

PROFIT STATEMENT

	£	£
Sales		10,200
Less: cost of sales	6,500	
depreciation of plant	1,700	8,200
Profit		2,000

BALANCE SHEET

	£	£
Plant (less depreciation)		6,400
Stock	3,000	
Debtors	2,100	
Bank	2,300	
	7,400	
Less: creditors	3,000	4,400
		10,800
Opening capital		8,800
Profit retained		2,000
		10,800

These statements therefore reveal that MN has been profitable during the period to the extent of a historic cost figure of £2,000, and that his net worth is £10,800 at the end of it. However, an alternative treatment could produce significantly different figures – that is, if the repairs were treated as an operating expense and not as a depreciable asset. That is:

PROFIT STATEMENT

	£	£
Sales		10,200
Less: cost of sales (s)	9,000	
depreciation of plant (t)	1,450	10,450
Loss		(250)

BALANCE SHEET

	£	£
Plant (less depreciation) (u)		4,150
Stock	3,000	
Debtors	2,100	
Bank	2,300	
	7,400	

Less: creditors	3,000	4,400
		8,550
Opening capital		8,800
Less: loss for period		(250)
		8,550

In this case, an alternative treatment of a payment (operating expense or depreciable asset) can transform a £2,000 profit into a £250 loss, and a £10,800 net worth into a figure of £8,550. Both treatments attempt presumably to reflect the reality of the payment of £2,500. It is open to argument as to which is the appropriate method. Both raise doubts about the degree of distortion of the underlying reality that exists for the user. It is essential, therefore, that such distortions are avoided if a proper understanding by the user is to be achieved. In other words, the method of accounting and reporting should be one that eliminates distortions if at all possible.

USER DECISIONS

Reported accounting information bears upon various decisions affecting its users – that is, the need for such information stems from the formulation of a decision in which alternatives require to be assessed, and about which knowledge does not exist currently. Thus, the purpose of useful, relevant, corresponding, measured and comprehensible information about an entity is that it should relate to the decisions of the user. This means that the nature of decisions should be taken into account when preparing accounting information – that is, it is not the user per se who is the reason for the latter being prepared; it is his decisions that provide the impetus. For example:

OP is an investor who is considering investing in certain stock market investments. He is uncertain as to which investments his available funds should be directed. What he requires is relevant information concerning the available alternatives. The information he obtains should do more than merely relate to him in his generally vague role as an investor. Instead, it ought to be concerned with providing him with knowledge that can be fed into his decision model – in no way predetermining the decision but capable of influencing it by improving his knowledge of the alternatives concerned.

The investment decision is largely concerned with the prediction of future dividend flows and eventual investment realization proceeds. Thus OP should be anxious to obtain accounting information that aids his prediction of these matters for the entities in which he is considering investment. Information to aid prediction is therefore a key part of the role of accounting, whether this is predicting dividend flows (as in the case of OP), funds available to repay loans, funds available to meet wage increases, or cash flows generated by increased prices. Obviously, the detail of decisions will vary according to the report user, but they all have one thing in common – they require the user to predict, and the available information must relate to the latter function if it is to be useful.[5]

SUMMARY

Some time has been spent in this chapter on the fundamentals of financial accounting and reporting. Because they are essential to any such system, and therefore to that of cash flow accounting, it is useful to summarize them before proceeding further.

ACCOUNTING FUNDAMENTALS

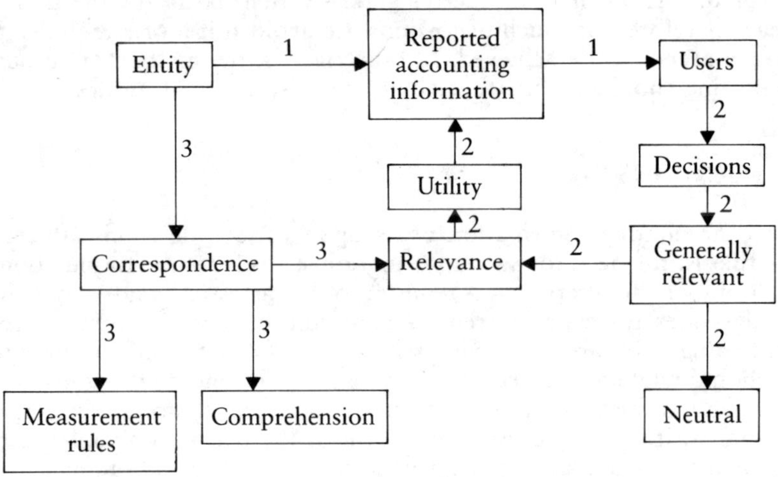

(1) Economic activity is conducted within a defined entity. Persons external to the latter have an interest in such activity with a view to making decisions concerning their relationships with the entity. However, they lack the knowledge needed from a direct experience of the activity in which they are interested. Reported accounting information is required to provide a surrogate for this direct experience.

(2) Reported accounting information must be useful to those persons identified as potential users in terms of their ascertainable decisions. In order to satisfy the objective of utility, the information must be relevant to these decisions – but only in a general sense in order not to anticipate specific decisions and lose necessary neutrality.

(3) In addition, in order to be relevant and useful, the reported accounting information should correspond to the reality of the economic activity of the entity. It must be measured according to generally acceptable and appropriate measurement rules, and dis-

closed in a manner and form that will be comprehensible to the identified users.

It is within this framework that cash flow accounting will be discussed further. Before this, however, the following chapter will examine the present-day system of external financial reporting as a basis for the detailed discussion on cash flow accounting.

CHAPTER 3 Traditional system of accounting

CONCEPT OF PROFIT

The current system of accounting for purposes of external financial reporting is based on certain traditional measurement ideas and rules that appear to have achieved general acceptance by accounting producers and users – despite growing and varied criticism and doubts concerning their validity.

The first point to make is that such accounting is centred firmly on the notion of measuring and disclosing a periodic measure of income or profit. This familiar man-made construct appears to be crucial to the assessment of the financial performance of business entities. Profit is regarded as an indicator of financial achievement and as a signal of success. Other things being equal, the greater the level of profitability, the higher the achievement and success. Profits thus appear to have become measures that can be related to the assessment of financial performance and, therefore, to various business and investment decisions associated with the latter – for example, dividends, taxation, managerial bonuses, wage increases and price changes.[6] In summary, profits are the lynch-pin of the capitalist system of economic enterprise.

But the concept of profit depends for its existence on other concepts, conventions, practices and judgments that cause it to be an exceedingly complex and misunderstood financial measure. It is certainly not one that should be taken for granted without thought or definition.

ACCOUNTING CAPITAL

Periodic profit is usually taken to represent an increase in the well-being, well-offness, or worth of the person or entity to which it is attributed.[7] Notions of such vagueness as well-being, etc., however, require to be defined more precisely for accounting purposes, and are generally taken to mean that accounting capital represents the assets of the person or entity after allowing for related liabilities.[8] For instance:

QR has total assets at the beginning of a period of £22,000 and related liabilities of £8,000. The respective end-of-period figures are £32,000 and £9,000. Thus, his opening and closing capital, and resultant periodic profit would be as follows:

	£
Opening capital (a)	14,000
Closing capital (b)	23,000
Periodic profit	9,000

This calculation assumes that there has been no change during the period in the capital contributed by QR, and there has been no distribution made. QR can therefore be said to be 'better off' by £9,000 at the end of the period compared with his position at the beginning of it. But much depends on two related factors – the valuation method attributed to the assets underlying capital; and the capital maintenance rule applied to the increment or decrement in capital valuation to determine profit. Each of these points will now be discussed.[9]

ACCOUNTING VALUATION

If accounting capital is defined largely in terms of the assets of the person or entity concerned at a particular point of time, it is a relatively common-sense point to make that these assets require to be identified and valued in order to get the aggregate datum termed capital. The concept of value for accounting purposes, however, is not a straightforward issue. Much depends, first, on what is identified as an asset; and, secondly, which of several available valuation systems is applied to the identified assets. For example:

Assuming the previous figures for QR, further assume that the capital data are valuations of 4 motor vehicles aggregated with a bank balance. No other assets have been identified for accounting purposes. The system of valuation adopted is historic or original cost, allowing for depreciation over the useful lives of the vehicles concerned. Thus:

BALANCE SHEETS

	Opening £	*Closing* £
Motor vehicles at cost (c)	40,000	44,000
Less: aggregate depreciation (d)	20,000	26,000
	20,000	18,000
Bank balance	2,000	14,000
	22,000	32,000
Less: creditors	8,000	9,000
	14,000	23,000
Capital	10,000	10,000
Profits retained	4,000	13,000
	14,000	23,000

During the period, one vehicle costing £10,000 was written off. Its net cost at the beginning of the period was £5,000, as were those of the other 3 vehicles. A further vehicle was purchased during the period for £14,000. Each remaining vehicle was depreciated by one quarter of its original cost. In other words, the assets of QR, and his capital and periodic profit, were measured using a system of valuation based on the allocation of historic costs. For purposes of obtaining a capital aggregation, much depends on when those costs were incurred, and the method of allocating periodically the recorded data. Different allocation procedures would produce different series of valuations for the vehicles, different capital data and, consequently, different profit figures.

Assume the vehicles were written off over five instead of four periods. The balance sheet of QR would be:

BALANCE SHEETS

	Opening £	*Closing* £
Motor vehicles at cost (e)	40,000	44,000
Less: aggregate depreciation (f)	16,000	20,800
	24,000	23,200
Bank balance	2,000	14,000
	26,000	37,200
Less: creditors	8,000	9,000
	18,000	28,200
Capital	10,000	10,000
Profits retained	8,000	18,200
	18,000	28,200

In other words, the profit of the period using the alternative variation of the historic cost basis would have been £10,200[g] rather than £9,000 using the first alternative basis. The difference between the two reflects that, although each uses historic costs, the net data achieved in this case are dependent totally on the allocation procedures applied to the gross costs.

Certain valuation bases are therefore allocation-based, and capital figures are influenced by this combination of valuation and allocation (the latter being a process dependent on subjective judgment). Historic cost is one such system. Another would be replacement cost in which assets are accounted for using replacement prices. For example:

Assume the data for QR in which the motor vehicles were written off over four periods. Also assume that their replacement price was £12,500 each (at the beginning of the period) and £15,500 each (at its end). The replacement cost balance sheet would be as follows:

BALANCE SHEETS

	Opening £	*Closing* £
Motor vehicles at replacement cost (h)	50,000	62,000
Less: aggregate depreciation (i)	25,000	38,750
	25,000	23,250
Bank balance	2,000	14,000
	27,000	37,250
Less: creditors	8,000	9,000
	19,000	28,250
Capital	10,000	10,000
Profits retained (including revaluations) (j)	9,000	18,250
	19,000	28,250

On a replacement cost basis, therefore, QR has accumulated total profits of £9,250[k], instead of £9,000 under the equivalent historic cost system, and total capital at the end of the period is £28,250 compared with £23,000. The allocation procedure of depreciating the vehicles over four periods has remained constant; the variable in this instance has been the valuation basis.

The situation can be varied still further by using a valuation basis which is not dependent on allocations – that is, which adopts prices determined in the market place and which do not require accountants to make subjective inter-period allocations of data. The system referred to involves sale prices.[10] For example:

Again, assume the previous situation of QR except that his 4 vehicles had a beginning-of-period sale price of £4,000 each and a closing price of £1,800 for each of the three oldest and £8,000 for that purchased during the period. QR's balance sheet position would be as follows:

BALANCE SHEETS

	Opening £	*Closing* £
Motor vehicles at sale price (l)	16,000	13,400
Bank balance	2,000	14,000
	18,000	27,400
Less: creditors	8,000	9,000
	10,000	18,400
Capital	10,000	10,000
Profits retained (including revaluations) (m)	—	8,400
	10,000	18,400

Placing the form of accounting on a sale price basis has changed the financial position and profitability of QR. The profit in total for the period is £8,400, compared with £9,000 under historic cost accounting and £9,250 under replacement cost accounting (assuming the same allocation methods for the latter two systems).

Summarizing to date, therefore, QR can produce the following profit and capital figures using valuation bases involving, respectively, historic costs, replacement costs, and sale prices:

	Opening capital £	*Closing capital* £	*Profit* £
Historic cost accounting	14,000	23,000	9,000
Replacement cost accounting	19,000	28,250	9,250
Sale price accounting	10,000	18,400	8,400

Remembering that at least the first two systems can be further 'flexed' by varying the allocation procedures connected with asset depreciation, it becomes rapidly apparent that a system of financial reporting centred around the concept of profit (and related capital) is one in which a great deal of flexibility can be entertained.

CAPITAL MAINTENANCE

This potential flexibility is extended further when the issue of capital maintenance is introduced. Capital maintenance is the term used to denote the function concerned with making a decision about how much of the periodic capital increment or decrement is to be treated as profit and how much should be regarded as capital to be retained in the business to maintain the latter in terms of the beginning-of-the-period situation.

Much depends on the judgment that is made as to what opening capital is to be maintained at the end of the period. There is general agreement that it should be the opening capital that is required to be maintained before determining periodic income. But there is little agreement as to what that opening capital should represent. Should it be money (that is, the number of £s represented); purchasing power (that is, generalized in the sense of some 'basket of goods and services' that could be purchased with it); or physical assets (that is, the structure of assets determining operating capability but represented in financial terms)?[11]

The first-mentioned system is essentially that which conforms with the law relating to capital, profits and distributions. Assuming no capital receipts and repayments during the period, a certain amount of monetary capital existed at the beginning of the period, and this is required to be maintained if its owner is not to be worse off by the period-end. In the case of QR, his opening monetary capital was £14,000 and this would be the figure to be maintained. By the end of the period, his monetary capital had risen to £23,000 and the additional monetary increment of £9,000 can be regarded as profit. The same principles can be applied to each of the replacement cost and sale price situations – that is, if the capital figures concerned are regarded as sums of money to be maintained.

However, only in the case of sale prices does this make sense. The monetary meaning of the historic cost capital aggregate is obscure, to say the least. It represents the aggregation of a mixture of past costs that cannot be said to denote worth or wealth other than as a figure of capital invested piece-meal in the past. It certainly cannot be taken to represent a summation of the current value of capital. Nor does the addition of various current replacement costs cause a capital figure to be produced that has any obvious monetary meaning other than as an aggregate of replacement costs should all the assets concerned be replaced at the balance sheet date. This leaves the aggregation of sale prices – in this case, at least the capital figure can be taken to represent the cash available to QR should the assets be realized and his liabilities paid at the time of reporting. It therefore does describe a potential sum of money, and profit can be taken to be an increase in that potential sum. The other two systems do not produce capital increments that provide profit with a sensible monetary meaning because the dependent capital data lack the latter condition – what does a net increase in allocated historic or replacement costs actually mean in financial as distinct from arithmetical terms? An answer is difficult to find. The worth of an object is not usually determined in terms of its past or current cost – usually it is equated with present value or sale price when it is being considered from the point of view of the person or entity holding it.

The maintenance of capital in purchasing power terms creates similar problems regarding the meaning of capital and its related derivative of profit. For example:

Assume the original historic cost situation of QR, and that the general price index was standing at 100 at t_1, 110 at t_2, 121 at t_3 and 133 at t_4. Further assume the period being reported on in purchasing power terms is t_3 to t_4, and that the earliest vehicles were all bought at t_1 when business commenced with an opening capital of £10,000. The latest vehicle was purchased immediately following t_3.

The financial positions in terms of purchasing power at t_3 and t_4 would be as follows ($£_p$ is a unit of purchasing power and the translation process is that which is generally recognised for these purposes):

BALANCE SHEETS

	Opening $£_p(t_3)$	*Closing* $£_p(t_4)$
Motor vehicles (n)	48,400	55,288
Less: aggregate depreciation (o)	24,200	33,772
	24,200	21,516
Bank balance	2,000	14,000
	26,200	35,516
Less: creditors	8,000	9,000
	18,200	26,516

Capital (p)	12,100	13,300
Profits retained (q)	6,100	13,216
	18,200	26,516

Translating capital at t_3 into t_4 purchasing power terms, and comparing with t_4 capital, the capital increment to be termed profit in purchasing power terms becomes:

	$£_p(t_4)$
Closing capital (t_4 terms)	26,516
Less: opening capital (t_4 terms) (r)	20,005
Profit	6,511

But what does such a profit mean or represent? It is based on a translation of net allocated historic costs. These are now described in the same measurement terms – generalized purchasing power at t_4. It therefore represents the net change in allocated historic costs after elimination of the distortion caused by using different measurement units in the original figure of money profit of £9,000. But the purchasing power equivalent of 6,511 generalized purchasing power units does not appear to be any more informative to the potential user than is the £9,000 increase in historic costs.

The same can be said of the equivalent replacement cost purchasing power data. With the assets in such a system already expressed in current purchasing power terms because of the use of current replacement prices, the balance sheet position in purchasing power terms is as follows, assuming the same index changes applied to the historic cost data:

BALANCE SHEETS

	Opening	*Closing*
	$£_p(t_3)$	$£_p(t_4)$
Motor vehicles	50,000	62,000
Less: aggregate depreciation	25,000	38,750
	25,000	23,250
Bank balance	2,000	14,000
	27,000	37,250
Less: creditors	8,000	9,000
	19,000	28,250
Capital (s)	12,100	13,300
Profits retained (including revaluations) (t)	6,900	14,950
	19,000	28,250

As the opening capital is in purchasing power terms at t_3, it requires to be further translated into t_4 terms for purposes of determining periodic profit after maintaining capital in current purchasing power terms. Thus:

	$£_p(t_4)$
Closing capital (t_4 terms)	28,250
Less: opening capital (t_4 terms) (u)	20,884
Profit	7,366

Profit is therefore measured as the increase in allocated replacement costs suitably adjusted to allow for the deterioration in the value of the money unit by 10%. However, although capital and profit have been described in so-called 'real' terms, their meaning must still be determined with reference to aggregations of replacement costs. The question must still be asked as to what these aggregations mean, and what the changes in the latter are intended to convey – with or without a capital maintenance adjustment in terms of purchasing power? An adequate answer is difficult to find.

Allowing for purchasing power capital maintenance procedures with the sale price model does not present such a problem. As it is based upon capital aggregations that appear to have a monetary meaning (sometimes described as command over resources, with capital as a 'pool' of monetary funds available to acquire resources),[12] the application of purchasing power adjustments is equally valid in order to ensure a proper comparison of capital data when deriving a measure of periodic profit. The latter, once determined in current purchasing power terms, represents the real increase in the entity's command over resources as described in realized and realizable price changes.

Applying the general index changes used above to the previously described sale price example, the following purchasing power-adjusted figures can be derived:

BALANCE SHEETS

	Opening $£_p(t_3)$	*Closing* $£_p(t_4)$
Motor vehicles at sale price	16,000	13,400
Bank balance	2,000	14,000
	18,000	27,400
Less: creditors	8,000	9,000
	10,000	18,400
Capital (v)	12,100	13,300
Profits retained (including revaluations) (w)	(2,100)	5,100
	10,000	18,400

Capital at t_3 now required to be translated into purchasing power terms at t_4 using the index movement of 121 to 133. This enables a comparison of opening and closing capital to be made in the same measurement terms:

	$£_p(t_4)$
Closing capital (t_4 terms)	18,400
Less: opening capital (t_4 terms) (x)	10,992
Profit	7,408

Profit in real terms is therefore $£_p$7,408, and this represents the additional purchasing power accruing to QR during the period in the form of realized or realizable cash flows (sale prices being potential cash flows). This can have meaning for the report user because the capital maintenance adjustment is compatible with the valuations that have proceeded it.

The question of applying capital maintenance procedures in financial terms has been discussed already – maintenance being undertaken either in terms of money or purchasing power. A further approach requires to be discussed, and this concerns the school of thought that regards capital as a collection of physical resources, either in terms of specific assets or their operating capability. The philosophy behind this approach is of the entity as a going concern and the requirement to ensure this continuity by preserving its physical assets.[13]

In the previously explained case of QR this means that, as he commenced the period with 4 vehicles, then profit should be determined having allowed for the maintenance of capital by the end of the period in terms of 4 vehicles. Accounting in terms of replacement costs is the system associated usually with the physical capital approach – profit being determined having accounted for assets consumed in terms of replacement costs, and not including revaluation surpluses and deficits (generally described as holding gains and losses).[14] Thus, in the case of QR, profit after physical capital maintenance would be as follows, assuming nil proceeds for the vehicle written off and a £14,000 cash purchase for the replacement vehicle:

PROFIT STATEMENT

	£	£
Sales less operating costs (y)		25,000
Less: replacement cost depreciation (z)	15,500	
loss on write off of vehicle (aa)	6,250	21,750
Profit		3,250

In other words, of the total change in profits retained of £9,250, £3,250 can be regarded as the current period profit after allowing for the replacement of assets consumed and, thus, for physical capital maintenance. The remaining £6,000 would comprise revaluation surpluses (£10,500)[bb] minus backlog depreciation (£4,500)[cc].[15] But the problem with physical capital maintenance is its relevance in a situation that is not static – that is, when the nature and structure of the entity is changing, and when technology results in non-identical replacement of assets. So much depends on these variables as to make physical capital maintenance an elusive procedure to practice.

In summary to date, therefore, the accounting function of capital maintenance causes the determination of periodic profit to be a relatively flexible and complex procedure. The following profit figures have been determined, utilizing either a financial capital or a physical capital approach (as explained in the previous sections):

Valuation basis	*Financial capital maintenance*		*Physical capital maintenance*
	Money	*Purchasing power*	
	£	$£_p$	£
Historic cost	9,000	6,511	—
Replacement cost	9,250	7,366	3,250
Sale price	8,400	7,408	—

The variability of profit as a potential guide to entity performance should be a matter of concern to both producer and user of accounting information. What is QR's profit under these circumstances? The answer is plainly one of several alternatives – not one of a single profit datum but one of many. This makes profit measurement a variable answer to the problem of supplying useful and relevant accounting information.

COST ALLOCATION

Valuation and capital maintenance are two of the main causes of potential variability in the measurement of profit (and, necessarily, financial position). As previously mentioned, so too is allocation – that is, vary the allocation procedure (such as depreciation), and costs are changed, and the matching of the latter with sales revenue produces differing profits (the greater the allocation to be matched with revenue, the smaller the profit; and vice versa). There thus appears to be a potentially substantial variety of profit data based on the same circumstances and dependent on the accounting judgments of allocation, valuation and capital maintenance applied. One thing, however, remains constant and independent of these accounting judgments, and that is the realized cash flow underlying the profit and financial position figures. This is the 'bed-rock' that cannot be flexed because of inter-period allocations, and valuation and capital maintenance decisions – because none of these matters pertain to such cash flow measurements.

In the case of QR used to illustrate the previous discussions, the cash flow position has changed as follows during the period concerned:

	£
Opening bank balance	2,000
Closing bank balance	14,000
Increase in cash during period	12,000
Comprising:	
Cash from operations (dd)	26,000
Less: payment for new vehicle	14,000
	12,000

These figures ought to be indisputable – they are devoid of time-period allocations (no depreciation is necessary because each payment is treated as a cash outflow of the period in which it took place); valuations (realized cash flows are not concerned with positions in time); and capital maintenance (for the same reason as with valuation). In other words, it is a system of straightforward information that has the considerable advantage of avoiding the complex issues of conventional accounting based on traditional measures of periodic profit and related financial position.

CHAPTER 4 Testing the traditional system

ACCOUNTING FUNDAMENTALS

The system of cash flow accounting introduced briefly at the end of the last chapter is the main subject of this text. It will be described in far greater detail throughout the remaining chapters. Meantime, several questions must be asked of the traditional system of accounting specified in its various forms in Chapter 3. Answers to these questions provide grounds for considering cash flow accounting as an important alternative to the traditional system.

The questions to be asked are focused largely on the basic criteria of external accounting and reporting which were identified in Chapter 2. In particular, these concern the utility and relevance of measures of profit and related financial position to report users; the correspondence of the latter financial results to the economic reality of the reporting entity; and the comprehensibility of these results to report users.

The most fundamental question is how useful and relevant the various measurements of profitability and financial position are to the users of financial reports generally, and their decision models particularly. An analysis of this issue can only be made in general terms (that is, in relation to a group of users and to a common decision model for that group, rather than to a specific user and to a particular decision of that person). To narrow the analysis to the latter situations would be in conflict with the criteria of general relevance and information neutrality, and it would also be unreal because of lack of firm evidence regarding the specific behaviour of individual users.[16] Much of what is written about users is the conventional and, usually, widely accepted wisdom concerning their general decision models.

The other criteria consider, first, how well each of the main profit-orientated measurements correspond to the economic activities of the reporting entity (and particularly question the accounting rules adopted); and, second, the degree to which the information is capable of being understood by its recipients.

The main user groups that will be considered in this chapter are owners (including sole traders, partners and shareholders; and their advisors); lenders (including bankers; and also including expert advisors); suppliers (including trade associations); employees (including trade unions); customers (including consumer associations); and government agencies (such as the tax authorities). The list is not intended to be complete – merely to reflect the main user groupings and also to include persons who may be acting on behalf of users or providing expert services for the latter (for example, stockbrokers and financial journalists).

OWNERS

The first user group to be examined is that of owners. These persons contribute capital to the reporting entity in various ways, depending on the nature of the entity. Capital may be introduced initially in the form of lump sums of cash and/or by the donation of non-monetary assets. Similar contributions may be made at future dates, but the main funding by owners throughout the life of the entity is in the form of profit retentions. Owners take the greatest investment risk in business – they are the last in the queue when profits are distributed and when capital is repaid. Their investment is therefore the most permanent of all the contributions made to the development of the entity.

As owners (as distinct from managers), the information that is most required is that concerned with distributions. If owners' capital is to remain within the entity, the major concern is the return to be gained from making such an investment – that is, the reward for the risk taken. Typically, this reward takes the form of a cash distribution. Thus, the sole trader or partner will be anxious to know how much can be withdrawn from the entity in the form of salaries, interest on capital and personal drawings; and the shareholder will require information related to dividends.

This is not to say that owners are interested solely in distributions. They will also be concerned with matters such as the financial performance of the entity in terms of its profitability, and its viability in terms of financial position and future prospects. Each of these factors can be decomposed into various detailed items, but the essential point is that the topic of distributions is the end-point of all these considerations – that is, distributions are a reflection of and related to financial performance, position and prospects. The question in this context is how useful and relevant are the various measures of profit and financial position to the owner concerned with distributions. This can be best demonstrated by use of simple examples.

OWNERS AND HISTORIC COST INFORMATION

Suppose ST is in business buying and selling golf balls. At 1 January, his capital was £1,000, and was held in the form of a cash balance of that amount. During the year to 31 December, he buys balls for cash of £8,000 and sells them for cash of £10,000. He makes a distribution of £1,500 before 31 December. Assuming he has no stock, debtors or creditors at 31 December (and ignoring taxation), the following historic cost financial statements can be produced for the year to the latter date:

PROFIT STATEMENT

	£
Sales	10,000
Less: cost of sales	8,000
Profit	2,000
Less: distribution	1,500
Profit retained	500

BALANCE SHEET

	£
Bank	1,500
Capital	1,000
Profit retained	500
	1,500

In this particular case, owing to the lack of non-monetary assets and other liabilities, profitability and liquidity are synonymous. ST can view the profit statement as a means of assessing profitability and liquidity, and his knowledge concerning the distribution made will include information on both factors – that is, he knows that the distribution of £1,500 was justified in terms of both available profit and cash flow. The profit statement is also a cash flow statement. In addition, the balance sheet reveals an apparently healthy position that has been capable of sustaining the payment of a distribution of £1,500.

Thus, in this simple case, the historic cost statements do provide useful and relevant information concerning the needs of the owner. They correspond reasonably to the economic events that occurred in the entity during the year to 31 December – golf balls were sold for £10,000, having been purchased for £8,000; and additional cash was generated of £2,000, of which £1,500 was distributed. This can be seen in the related funds statement:

FUNDS STATEMENT

	£
Source of funds	
Profit before distribution	2,000
	£
Application of funds	
Distribution	1,500
Increase in bank account (a)	500
	2,000

No subjective judgments have been involved, and each of the statements can be said to be factual. They can also be said to be reasonably comprehensible. But what if the simplifying assumptions are relaxed? Will the historic cost statements be as relevant and useful to ST, correspond as well with economic reality, and be understood? The following example introduces the complexity of working capital and fixed asset data to the above illustration (stock £2,000, debtors £1,000, creditors £200, plant £1,000, depreciation £100), and further assumes a distribution payment of £1,500.

PROFIT STATEMENT

	£
Sales	10,000
Less: cost of sales (b)	6,000
	4,000
Less: depreciation of plant (c)	100
	3,900
Less: distribution	1,500
Profit retained	2,400

BALANCE SHEET

	£	£
Plant (less depreciation) (c)		900
Stock		2,000
Debtors		1,000
		3,900
Less: creditors	200	
bank (e)	300	500
		3,400
Capital		1,000
Profits retained		2,400
		3,400

FUNDS STATEMENT

	£	£
Source of funds		
Profit before depreciation		4,000
Uses of funds		
Purchase of plant		1,000
Increase in working capital:		
Stock (f)	2,000	
Debtors (g)	1,000	
(Creditors) (h)	(200)	2,800

Distribution	1,500
	5,300
Decrease in bank balance (i)	1,000
Increase in bank overdraft	300
	1,300

In other words, historic cost profits before depreciation of £4,000 (£3,900 after depreciation) were more than sufficient to cover the distribution of £1,500, but the effects of the purchase of plant of £1,000 and the increase in working capital of £2,800 also have to be considered.

The balance sheet reveals a financial position that is not unhealthy following the distribution. Working capital (including the bank overdraft) is a positive £2,500.[j] Capital has increased by £2,400 (the retained profit). However, the funds statement hints at the inadequacy of ST relying on the profit statement and balance sheet to assess distribution and related factors. £1,300 of cash has been required to fund all the entity's needs – £1,000 being the opening bank balance consumed and £300 being the further accumulated bank overdraft. This can be more clearly seen in a cash flow statement:

CASH FLOW STATEMENT

	£
Cash inflow	
Operating cash flow*	1,200
Bank borrowing	300
Decrease in bank balance	1,000
	2,500
Cash outflow	
Purchase of plant	1,000
Distribution	1,500
	2,500

	£
*	
Sales (k)	9,000
Less: purchases (l)	7,800
	1,200

What the historic cost statements therefore have failed to reveal to ST when he is considering the distribution is that the realized profit of £4,000 has an equivalent periodic cash flow of £1,200 – a figure that is less than the distribution of £1,500. The difference of £300 has been funded by bank overdraft. Thus, the historic cost statements (including the funds statement) have been less than complete in the information given to ST. If he wishes to consider profitability and liquidity in relation to the distribution, the traditional set of historic cost financial statements does not appear to be as useful or relevant as might be expected – certainly the profit statement is misleading in reporting a realized profit of £4,000 that has provided a positive cash flow of only £1,200; the balance sheet reveals a financial position that is arguably healthier than may be the case (so much depends on the realizability of the plant, stock and debtors – will they realize the historic cost aggregate of £3,900?); and the funds statement only hints at the underlying cash flow for it is dependent on the reporting of the £4,000 realized profit as the main source of funding.

If, as has been argued above, the traditional set of statements is less than full in its information on the reporting entity for the owner, can they be said to correspond to the entity's activities and are they comprehensible? In relation to correspondence, they appear to fall short of the mark. First, they do not easily reveal factual information concerning, for example, cash in and cash out (only the funds statement gives part of this information). Second, they obscure factual data by use of judgmental data relating to working capital and fixed assets. Factually, stock costing £2,000 remains unsold at 31 December, but can this be said to be a fair accounting statement of stock at that date when cost relates to the date(s) of purchase and not to the reporting date? Factually, fixed assets were purchased for £1,000 during the year, but is the unallocated figure of £900 at 31 December a datum fairly representing financial position at that date, and does the £100 depreciation expense describe a meaningful change in these assets since acquisition?

On all these issues, the answers would appear to be negative and suggest that the historic cost statements do not conform entirely with what happened either during the period or at the end of it. They are a mixture of past fact altered by subsequent judgments. Equally, it must be argued that, for similar reasons, the historic cost figures do not provide comprehensible information. There is the danger of non-accounting users with a poor understanding of conventional accounting practice in particular believing that the realized profit figure of £4,000 has been realized in cash whereas £2,800 had been invested in working capital[m]; the depreciation expense of £100 represents a fall in value of that amount, and that £900 is the current value of the plant at 31 December; and that ST is 'better off' by £2,400 (the retained profit) compared with his opening position. These are all matters that could confuse and mislead the less-sophisticated user (and, arguably, some more sophisticated persons).[17]

In summary, therefore, historic cost statements provide out-of-date data regarding financial position, and report on realized profits that may not be available in cash. They depend on allocations such as depreciation and give no information regarding the realizability of assets being held. They do not correspond well with what has happened in the reporting entity, and they could be misunderstood. They lack information of direct utility and relevance when considering matters such distributions to owners.

OWNERS AND REPLACEMENT COST INFORMATION

The next step is to relax the assumption to date of price stability and consider current value alternatives to historic cost in relation to the needs of owners. The first case will deal with replacement costs and, as before, will utilize a figure example to illustrate the points being made. The previous situation of ST is used with the additional information that the replacement cost of sales was £7,500, stock at 31 December, £2,800, and plant at 31 December, £1,200. All other matters remain as for the historic cost example.

PROFIT STATEMENT

	£
Sales	10,000
Less: replacement cost of sales	7,500
	2,500
Less: replacement cost repreciation (n)	120
	2,380
Less: distribution	1,500
Profit retained	880

BALANCE SHEET

	£	£
Plant (less depreciation) (o)		1,080
Stock		2,800
Debtors		1,000
		4,880
Less: creditors	200	
bank	300	500
		4,380
Capital		1,000
Profits retained and revaluations:		
Profits retained	880	
Cost of sales (p)	1,500	
Stock (q)	800	
Plant (r)	200	3,380
		4,380

With unrealized asset revaluations, etc., being bookkeeping entries for funds statement purposes, the relevant funds statement for ST remains as under the historic cost system. But what do the replacement cost statements tell him? First, he learns that the historic cost profit of £3,900 (before distribution) either overstates profitability (if a physical capital maintenance approach is adopted, replacement cost profit is £2,380) or understates it (if a financial capital approach is used, total replacement cost profit is £4,880)[s]. Either way, historic cost accounting has not taken into account certain changing prices and their effect on profitability and funding.

But are the replacement cost alternatives any more useful and relevant to ST? The physical capital profit before distribution of £2,380 suggests that the entity has been less profitable than under historic cost rules, and presumably that profits available for distribution are not as substantial as the historic cost model suggests. But it reveals nothing of the operational cash flow surplus realized of £1,200, and thus ST is no better informed as to liquidity than he was before. In addition, there is the confusion of at least two variants of replacement cost profit before distribution – £2,380 excluding realized and unrealized holding gains, and £4,880[t] including all such gains. It would therefore be exceedingly difficult to decide from these figures the level of profitability that should be used to determine distributions – should it be £2,380 thus conserving physical capital; or £4,880 with financial capital maintained? Both might lead to different distributions in a situation where liquidity was a constant.

Second, the replacement cost balance sheet gives the distinct impression of a stronger financial position than under historic cost accounting. Total replacement cost working capital is £3,300[u] rather than its historic cost equivalent of £2,500, and capital has increased by £3,380 instead of £2,400. But is ST's financial position on a replacement cost basis stronger than on a historic cost basis? The answer must be negative as the business situation and resources are identical under both systems. The only substantial differences between them concern revaluations of certain assets and the classification of holding and operating gains. Thus, the replacement cost balance sheet (and its related profit statement) could be confusing when related to distributions – they do not necessarily provide more relevant information for this purpose than do those dependent on historic cost data.

The next question to be asked is whether the replacement cost information corresponds with the economic reality of the entity it is purporting to describe. In this respect, they appear to be no better than their historic cost equivalents. Not only do they obscure the factual cash flow data that have arisen during the period, but they also rely on subjective allocations of equally subjective valuations. The replacement costs used do not have the factual merit of historic costs – they are based on the cost of replacement at the time of reporting. But replacement may not be made and, even if such a function eventually takes place, it may not be in identical or equivalent form. For example:

ST has purchased plant for £1,000. At the time of reporting, it is estimated that it has a replacement cost of £1,200. But replacement will not take place for a further 9 years (assuming a full life of 10 years), and it is difficult to envisage the nature of the replacement at that time – the plant may not be replaced; and, if it is not, a major question arises as to what the depreciation funds retained will have been used to finance. Even if there is replacement, it is impossible to say what the replacement will be. Similar problems also arise with stock and its possible replacement. Consequently, both the replacement cost-based profit statement and its related balance sheet contain data that do not correspond with reality.

The remaining question to be asked of replacement cost information is whether it is likely to be comprehensible. Much would obviously depend on the accounting knowledge of the individual user, but it is certainly not difficult to assume that there may be considerable problems for all users when attempting to interpret replacement cost financial statements. For example:

ST receives the replacement cost profit statement and balance sheet for the year to 31 December. In the profit statement, he reads that the profit before distribution is £2,380 (after deduction of various replacement costs), and he may take this to be a proper reflection of the entity's profitability for the period. However, it is only part of its realized profit of £3,900 (as revealed by historic cost accounting). The difference comprises the following data:

PROFIT STATEMENT

	£	£
Historic cost profit		3,900
Less: additional cost of sales (v)	1,500	
additional depreciation (w)	20	1,520
Replacement cost profit		2,380

In other words, what is happening in replacement cost accounting is that the realized profit of £3,900 is being split into two parts – the first representing the gains due to holding assets when prices changed (£1,520)[x] and the remainder being the gain on sale of the assets concerned (£2,380). In addition, the holding gains of £1,520 that have been realized can also be augmented by unrealized holding gains of £980[y] due to the revaluation of fixed assets and stock. Thus, in this example, profit can be one of the following alternatives (each stated as before distribution):

		£
(1)	Operating gain only (as above)	2,380

		£
(2)	Operating gain (as in (1))	2,380
	Holding gains (x)	1,520
	Historic cost profit	3,900

		£
(3)	Operating gain (as in (1))	2,380
	Holding gains (as in (2))	1,520
	Unrealized holding gains (y)	980
	Total gains	4,880

What then is the profit of the entity? It varies in this particular case by £2,500 depending on the treatment of holding gains, and even the realized profit can vary by £1,520, despite the fact that only £1,200 of the £3,900 total is available in cash form. This variability is a difficult matter for the experienced user to cope with – let alone the uninitiated user. Equally, the replacement cost balance sheet must contain comprehension problems. Total assets are described with a value of £4,880 – but what does this mean? It is not the original cost (arguably irrelevant but at least based on fact), and it is certainly not the sale price. Instead, it is a summation of various judgments concerning possible future replacement. This makes the capital situation as difficult to understand as that of profit. Particularly with regard to the treatment of holding gains, is the capital to be maintained to be £1,000 (the original capital), £3,500 (that including holding gains)[z], or £4,380 (that including all retained gains)[aa]? Each can be argued for but each results in a different interpretation of profitability and financial position. Hardly a situation to minimise confusion, and hardly one which will aid ST in his assessment of business performance and position generally, and the entity's distributions particularly.

OWNERS AND SALE PRICE INFORMATION

Perhaps then the sale price-based alternative can provide more useful information? In order to discuss it, the example of ST used throughout this chapter will be extended to include sale prices. In particular, the following additions to the basic historic cost data should be noted – the plant has a sale price of £700 at 31 December, and the stock at the same date would retail for £3,800. The undernoted financial statements result:

PROFIT STATEMENT

	£
Sales	10,000
Less: cost of sales	6,000
	4,000
Less: depreciation of plant (bb)	300
	3,700
Add: unrealized stock gains (cc)	1,800
	5,500
Less: distribution	1,500
Profit retained	4,000

BALANCE SHEET

		£
Plant		700
Stock		3,800
Debtors		1,000
		5,500
Less: creditors	200	
bank	300	500
		5,000
Capital		1,000
Profits retained		4,000
		5,000

Note: As before, the funds statement would be as in the system of historic cost accounting, bookkeeping entries due to revaluation and depreciation not affecting the flow of funds.

The above profit statement reveals a realized profit of £4,000 before depreciation (as in historic cost accounting) and thus also fails to disclose that only £1,200 of this is available in cash (the remaining £2,800 being invested in working capital). However, ST has some indication of realized and unrealized profit in sale price terms – he is informed of a £300 fall in the market value of his plant, and a potential profit of £1,800 to be realized on his period-end stock. Thus, total realizable profits amount to £5,500 and, after allowing for the £1,500 distribution made, the profit statement suggests that ST is £4,000 'better-off' in resource terms by the end of the period. The balance sheet confirms this in terms of asset data that describe 'better-offness' reasonably well – that is, in terms of sale prices that, when aggregated, provide a meaningful total representing the net cash or cash equivalent resources available to ST at that point in time. Thus, he is provided with information that could be of considerable potential to him when he is deciding on such matters as how much profit to distribute and how much to plough back (a realizable amount of £4,000 being available); whether or not to continue in business; and, if so, what form of business to be in (net realizable resources of £5,000 are available for this purpose). The discussion and contemplation of alternative courses of action for decision making purposes appear ideally suited for sale price-based systems of accounting because sale prices represent these choices well – existing resources having to be available and realized to distribute, wind-up, proceed in the existing format or switch to an alternative one. Sale prices represent cash equivalents, and these are the medium (when converted to cash) that allow alternative courses of action to be pursued.[18]

ST would therefore appear to have useful and relevant information in the form of sale price-based statements for purposes of choices and decisions he has to make, although he will also require additional information regarding cash flow if he is concerned to ascertain whether or not he has been both profitable and liquid. In this respect, it is important to note that cash flows and sale prices are both cash-orientated and this similarity will be explored in a later chapter. Meantime, the above financial statements ought to be examined in relation to the criteria of correspondence and comprehensibility.

So far as the former condition is concerned, it is reasonable to suggest that the sale price-based statements correspond to real-world matters – first, that goods were sold for £10,000 and these had cost £6,000 originally; and secondly, that the market value of the plant had fallen by £300 to £700 and that goods in stock costing £2,000 had a period-end sale price of £3,800. Thus, the situation is that, if ST had an orderly realization of his assets and repayment of his liabilities, he ought to be £4,000 better off than when he commenced business with his original capital of £1,000.

Turning to the question of comprehension, it does not appear unreasonable to make the suggestion that ST ought to be able to read his sale price financial statements and appreciate their meaning in terms of, for example, what has been achieved (the retained profit of £4,000), what has happened (the fall in price of plant of £300), and what could happen (the potential profit to be gained on the unsold stock of £1,800). In other words, such financial statements may accord with the popular if mistaken perception of other types of statement – that they are sale price-based.[19] This obviously would reduce the potential for confusion and misleading interpretations being made of them.

OTHER REPORT USERS

To date, each of the main systems of financial accounting have been discussed within the context of the needs of the owner of the business, ST. However, as earlier parts of this text have indicated, these financial statements may also be helpful to other interested parties – that is, lenders, suppliers, employees and government agencies. More specifically in this particular case, those interested persons would be ST's bank (the overdraft stands at £300), his creditors (£200 at the period-end), his employees (the example has omitted this consideration), and the tax authority (so far the question of tax has been ignored). Each of these potential users will be discussed in turn.

The banker has agreed overdraft facilities with ST up to a limit of £500. What should concern him at the period-end are four specific matters – first, how has the present overdraft of £300 been achieved and, in particular, what have the funds made available been used for; second, is the present security over the business assets of ST sufficient to cover a potential overdraft of £500 or, indeed, £300; third, is the overdraft of £300 likely to be extended to £500 or will it stabilize or reduce; and, fourth, will the interest costs be met and the overdraft be repaid eventually?

All of these matters can be seen to be related to the liquidity of ST's business. However, what the banker will receive by way of formal information from ST will be his historic cost-based financial statements for the period. These will inform him that the overdraft stands in the balance sheet as a liability of £300 (he already knows this from his own bank records and his knowledge is not increased in this respect). He will also see that the historic cost profit before depreciation is £4,000 and the retained profit is £2,400 – neither of which will inform him that only £1,200 was available in cash from ST's operations (a matter of crucial importance to the funding of the business). The balance sheet and funds statement will describe the purchase and depreciation of plant costing £1,000, but neither statement will reflect the sale price of plant that could be used as security for the overdraft. Equally, stock costing £2,000 does not state adequately the security available from a potential going concern sale price of £3,800. In other words, the historic cost-based statements of ST received by his banker appear to provide little information of direct relevance to his decisions, particularly with regard to liquidity matters.

The same conclusion can be reached with regard to replacement cost financial statements and the banker. By comparing sales of £10,000 with a replacement cost of £7,500, the profit before depreciation figure of £2,500 is nearer to the operational cash flow for the period of £1,200 than the historic cost equivalent of £4,000. But it remains as a profit-orientated figure, dependent on a cost allocation (stock), and not related specifically to a liquidity problem. Equally, the balance sheet figures for plant (£1,080) and stock (£2,800) do not relate to asset cover for security purposes.

These brief analyses suggest that, inter alia, the sale price-based statements of ST would provide information useful to banking decisions. This is not to suggest that such statements provide all the information required by the banker, but they are at least part of the information package required (statements of past and forecast cash flows would also be relevant to a banker concerned about business liquidity generally and potential overdraft facilities particularly). Not only would sale price statements be relevant, they would also correspond to matters which the banker will be examining – that is, the actual and potential generation of cash flow, and the availability of securable resources.

The same arguments can be applied to ST's suppliers. As with his banker, they will be concerned with matters of business liquidity although the time horizon for information and decisions may be shorter owing to the limited terms of credit, and the size of debt for an individual supplier may well be a fraction of the bank's commitment. Unfortunately, suppliers are not usually in the privileged position of bankers with regard to receipt of financial statements of businesses to which they are supplying. However, if they can receive information (as from publicly available files), they will inevitably find it to be historic cost-based in terms of profit and funds statements, and supporting balance sheets. Occasionally, for larger companies, information using mainly replacement cost data also may be included. But this, too, suffers from its lack of correspondence to liquidity matters.

ST's employee would be concerned to learn of the business' financial position and progress as this is linked clearly with security of employment, and prospects for wage-related benefits. The basic questions for the employee may well include, first, is the business likely to survive and provide continuing employment; and second, are funds likely to be available to meet wages bills (including any negotiable increases)? These are matters that relate to future periods and, thus, forecasts are ideally what are needed. But as these will not be available usually, the employee will require to utilize available information relating to past activity in order to judge these matters.

In practice, only employees of larger companies (and their representatives) receive financial information – usually in summarized form and based on historic costs. Although information relating to profitability may be of interest to the employee, it can be misleading with respect to decisions concerned with judgments of job and wage prospects. For example, to an employee of ST not versed in the complexities of financial accounting, the historic cost profit retained of £2,400 may appear to be funds available to meet wage increase demands. In fact, this figure merely represents a bookkeeping residue after cost allocations have been made for stock and plant depreciation, and a distribution has been deducted. In other words, the reported profit has already been distributed or reinvested as follows:

	£
Profit earned as per profit statement	4,000
Investment in increased working capital	2,800
Distribution made to ST	1,500
	4,300
Deficit of funding met by bank overdraft	300

Thus, if the employee is to be informed correctly about the availability of profit, he would require a statement of the above type or, alternatively, one based on an adequate correspondence with the underlying transactions and reasonably comprehensible to him. This could be in the form of a cash flow statement based on the above data (ignoring the use of the opening cash balance of £1,000 to purchase plant costing an identical amount):

	£
Cash flow realized from operations (dd)	1,200
Less: distribution made	1,500
Overdraft facility provided	300

Equally, the employee may be concerned to know what business resources are available to ST at the period-end to aid the continuity of the entity and its work-force. In this respect, the balance sheet described in historic cost terms does little to inform him about such availability – the net resources position is £3,400, whereas the current cash equivalent expressed in sale price terms is £5,000. It ought to be reasonably clear that the latter figure is a more meaningful indicator of resource availability than is the former. Sale prices are expressions of the cash that could be made available to acquire other resources. Historic costs are merely expressions of unallocated past costs. It also should be noted that the replacement cost figure for net resources at the period-end of £4,380 suffers from the same problem as its historic cost equivalent – it would not inform the employee of the availability of resources at the period-end for alternative courses of action.

The final potential external user to be discussed in this chapter is the tax authority as the most obvious example of a government agency that would be concerned to be informed about the financial affairs of ST's business. Specifically, the tax authority has the task of assessing the liability of tax of ST, and the basis for this is determined legally as his historic cost profit for the period concerned – that is, the historic cost profit of £4,000 will be the figure upon which the tax computation is built. In this respect, the tax authority will not be concerned with replacement cost or sale price figures and, instead, will concentrate on the historic cost statements as these are relevant to such an agency because of existing legal provisions. Matters such as the correspondence and comprehensibility of such information are secondary to this principle issue of utility. In fact, the tax authority will be concerned to identify those figures from the statements that it requires to use in order to comply with statutory provisions. It will also be concerned to ascertain the methods of cost allocation used to decide whether or not they are appropriate for purposes of tax computation – for example, those relating to the production of the period-end stock figure.

RELEVANCE OF COST-BASED INFORMATION

When examining the information needs of those persons potentially interested in receiving financial information about the business of ST, several matters appear to be reasonably clear. First, in most cases the historic and replacement cost models have deficiencies concerning relevance, correspondence and comprehensibility. The only possible exception to this general conclusion concerns the tax authority and its dependence on historic cost profit data. Second, all groups, with the exception of the tax authority, appear to require cash or cash equivalent data, and this would seem to be best provided through an accounting system dealing with cash flows and sale prices.

This is not to deny the possibly utility of other forms of financial accounting. To do so would be condeming systems such as historic cost and replacement cost accounting to a position they do not deserve. For example, historic cost accounting does attempt to reflect the realized profit for the period on the goods and services sold during that period. In doing this, it also attempts to avoid accounting for valuations and unrealized profits – that is, it tries to be as factual and objective as possible by means of the so-called convention of conservatism.[20] But to produce historic cost figures, certain judgments are essential.

For example, in the case of ST, the figure for profit before depreciation of £4,000 has been dependent on at least four judgments – the accounting for a closing stock of £2,000; the accrual of debtors of £1,000 and creditors of £200; and the depreciation of plant by £100.[21] Thus, the factual nature of the underlying cash flow of £1,200 has been altered as follows:

	Cash flow £	*Judgment* £	*Profit* £
Sales	9,000	1,000	10,000
Less: cost of sales	7,800	200	
		(2,000)	6,000
	1,200	2,800	4,000
Less: depreciation	—	100	100
	1,200	2,700	3,900

Thus, a considerable part of the accounting profit is comprised of subjective judgment. It cannot therefore be regarded as wholly factual and totally objective. But it does inform the user about profit as defined in terms of the historic cost/realization principles – that is, the judgments are confined to those related to past transactions, revenues and costs.

Similarly, it would be dangerous to argue that replacement cost-based financial statements are not useful and relevant. Although not apparently useful to the type of external report users examined in this chapter, replacement cost data could be beneficial to internal management concerned with levels of profitability sufficient to fund the replacement of assets consumed during a period of price instability. For example:

In the case of ST, the replacement cost statements reveal that, although the historic cost accounting profit before distribution amounted to £3,900, the replacement cost figure was £2,380. The reason for the difference was that the figure of £3,900 was essentially comprised of two elements as follows:

	£	£
Realized historic cost profit available for distribution without impairing the physical asset base of the business		2,380
Realized historic cost profit required to be retained in order to fund the increased cost of replacing:		
stock consumed (ee)	1,500	
plant utilized (ff)	20	1,520
Total historic cost profit		3,900

ST thus has information regarding the additional funding that has been required to replace resources consumed during the period, and thereby not available for distribution. In addition, the replacement cost balance sheet of ST informs him of the potential funding from profits which will be required to meet the additional cost of replacing the assets held at the balance sheet date and yet to be consumed:[22]

	£
Stock (gg)	800
Plant (hh)	180
Total unrealized increases in replacement cost	980

JUDGING THE TRADITIONAL SYSTEM

The analysis in this chapter has revealed several key problems related to financial accounting and reporting sytems that are centred on measurements of periodic profit and related capital:

(1) Although profit can be described generally as a measurement of how better off the individual or entity is at the end of a defined period compared with the position at its beginning, it has several specific meanings dependent on the methods of capital valuation and capital maintenance adopted. In others words, there is no unique meaning to be attributed to profit in practice, and this leaves it as a man-made financial indicator of considerable variety that has to be interpreted with a great deal of care and understanding.

(2) As different measures of profit can have differing meanings, so too can their related measures of capital and financial position. However, on occasion, it is extremely difficult to provide a satisfactory meaning for such aggregations – particularly in relation to those based on past or current cost allocations. Thus, it may be argued that aggregations of the latter measurements are not easily interpretable; and financial report users may attribute meanings which are inappropriate or misleading.

(3) The measurement for accounting purposes of profit and financial position is based usually on a mixture of factual transactions and subjective accounting judgments. The latter are unavoidable, but can be minimized. A major problem is finding a system that maximizes fact and minimizes judgment in order that subjectivity does not unnecessarily distort reality. Systems of accounting and reporting that utilize cost allocations are likely to contain these distortions, thus reducing their utility and relevance to report users because of their lack of correspondence and comprehensibility.

(4) There are several report user groups with generally identifiable decision models and related financial information needs. The models and needs can vary considerably, but, despite this, user groups have certain things in common – particularly relating to the actual and potential liquidity of the entity in which they have an interest. This suggests at the very least a need for cash and cash-equivalent information in addition to any need for cost allocation-based systems. In particular, cash flow and sale price reporting appear relevant. These systems have the added advantages of correspondence and

comprehensibility. It is to these matters that the remainder of this text will turn in the following chapters.

Before they are considered, however, it is important to make some related points concerning the traditional system of accounting based on cost allocation generally and historic costs particularly. First, a review of the accountancy literature over many years evidences the relative, if variable, dissatisfaction by accountants and report users with the historic cost accounting system. It is therefore unfair even to imply that it has not been challenged. It has been criticized on many occasions, and substantial changes have been made – for example, the introduction and implementation of a programme of prescribed accounting standards to reduce the flexibility in historic cost measurements due to cost allocation judgments such as stock valuations, fixed asset depreciation, and deferred taxation; accounting for current costs as a means of minimizing the misleading nature of historic cost accounting during a period of specific price instability; increased disclosure and explanations of accounting practices utilized in financial reports in order to inform report users more precisely of the procedures undertaken in preparing historic cost-based information; and funds statements to provide an explanation to users of overall movements in the financial position of the reporting entity (other than those described in the profit statement).

Second, despite each of these attempts at improving the state of external financial reporting, it remains a function that is subject to accounting complexity. None of the specific improvements mentioned above have aided this situation. The production of different profit figures in the same financial report requires a high level of accounting sophistication to interpret meaningfully.[23] Standardization has contained cost allocation-induced flexibility within only very broad limits, leaving a great deal of subjective judgment in the accounting and reporting process. Additional disclosures, although aimed at improving the reporting function for the report user, can cause him considerable problems when he attempts to identify the main financial messages contained in the detail of the individual financial statements.[24]

Third, to date, little more than lip-service has been paid in practice to the 'report user' approach to specifying the nature and content of published financial statements. Several studies have been produced that have outlined, in general terms only, the perceived needs of groups of potential users of financial statements.[25] However, there is little or no evidence that these writings have influenced significantly those persons and bodies responsible for prescribing accounting practices. Thus, current financial reporting practice appears to lack a sense of direction because of no explicit accounting objectives, uses and needs. This is not the approach of this text.

To summarize, therefore, traditional accounting practice has been subject to challenge, but this has been answered typically by practices that have tended to increase the complexity of financial reports for their users. In addition, the needs of the latter have not been acknowledged adequately in practice. These do not appear to be conditions ideally suited to provide report users with financial information that is useful and relevant;

corresponding to the underlying economic reality of the reporting entity; and understood by its users.

ALTERNATIVE SCHOOLS OF THOUGHT

Two particular schools of accounting thought in recent times have attempted to meet the needs of report users, and to comply with the aforementioned criteria. Although there are many arguments to be made for their separate adoption in practice, both schools have arisen in part because of the debate and subsequent doubts relating to the subjectivity of cost allocations in traditional accounting. The schools are, respectively, sale price accounting (SPA), which is based on sale prices,[26] and cash flow accounting (CFA), which utilizes cash flows.[27] Both attempt to avoid cost allocation-induced judgments but, more important, both aim to provide financial information that meets the needs of identifiable user groups. They also have the objective of reporting information that is as factual and comprehensible as possible.

SPA and CFA usually have been advocated by their supporters as separate systems of external accounting and reporting. Arguments have been presented for one or the other but, only recently, has any significant attempt been made to link the two systems in terms of a unified function of cash-based accounting and reporting.[28] In fact, as the next chapter will describe, both SPA and CFA are parts of this single system, and this text is aimed at describing, explaining and analysing it in detail.

CHAPTER 5 A unified system of cash flow reporting

REALIZED AND UNREALIZED CASH FLOWS

Previous chapters in this text have indicated that various report-user groups could benefit considerably from the reporting of information describing entity cash flows and related resources. It is now time to draw these strands together to present a unified argument for a cash-based system of accounting with cash flows and sale prices as the basic ingredients. Such a combined system utilizes practices developed under the separate labels of CFA and SPA, but the emphasis will be on a total system of cash flow reporting (CFR). Individual cases can and are made for CFA and SPA but, as this text will argue, they are essentially sub-sets of CFR, and the case should be made for the latter system as a whole. From this case, however, it will become apparent that CFA and SPA arguments are consistent and compatible with one another.

Before proceeding to the detail of the argument for CFR, it is essential that the reader is introduced to the system by means of a quantified example. This should provide an appreciation of the structure of the system, and thereby indicate the part each sub-set has to play in satisfying the information needs of most of the identifiable user groups. First, however, a preliminary explanation of the system is given.

CFR aims to report on both actual and potential cash flows. To report on one and not the other would be to provide an incomplete picture of cash flows. CFR should therefore contain statements relating to realized cash flows (a matter that is identified usually as the function of CFA in its ex post state) and realizable cash flows (which is typically the focus of SPA with sale prices representing cash equivalents). In order to provide an articulating reporting set, it is necessary to produce a statement of financial position describing the net asset position of the entity in realized and realizable terms (again, this is usually seen as the function of SPA). Finally, it is possible to complete the system by providing a statement of overall change in the financial position of the entity (thereby reflecting all actual and potential cash flow changes accounted for under CFA and SPA).

The complete system therefore contains four major statements, each of which will require consideration of the realizability of the reporting entity's net assets and resultant cash flows. Realizability is fundamental to the system because it enables the report user to distinguish net assets and cash flows which are realized (that is, those that exist in the form of cash as a result of cash flow transactions) from those that are unrealized (that is, those that exist in the form of the cash equivalent terms of sale prices). In this sense, realized items reflect cash and cash flows that have been achieved; realizable items reflect potential achievement in cash terms.

CFR depends on the above distinctions and, in order to reflect them in accounting and reporting, the classification of assets and liabilities is altered from that used in conventional accounting practice. The latter adopts classifications of assets and liabilities that naively describe realizability (in the case of assets) and payability (in the case of liabilities). However, it is doubtful if these conventions succeed completely in the implied aim. Many items of stock and work-in-progress, for example, may not be realizable in their existing state, raising doubts as to their current asset classification. Equally, fixed assets such as motor vehicles may be immediately realizable and call into question their conventional classification.

ASSET AND LIABILITY CLASSIFICATIONS[29]

Thus, it is being argued as a background to the financial statements to be described later in this chapter that a new approach must be made to conventional asset and liability classification. Assets should be classed according to their realizability in terms of an orderly liquidation – that is, as if the entity was adapting sensibly to changing circumstances.[30] In particular, these classifications should reflect the marketability of the assets concerned, but not the realization intentions of entity management. In order to obtain factual information relating to sale prices, it is necessary to seek those that exist in an identifiable market – even if this is a limited market. In this way, the accounting characteristic of correspondence is adhered to, and the required accounting data are determined without value judgments being imposed by the producer of financial statements. If a sale price does not exist, it would be proper to account for the asset concerned with a zero cash equivalent because this would reflect its financial condition at the time of reporting.

In addition, it would contravene the objectivity of the accounting process, and the factual quality of the information being reported, if management's intentions or expectations regarding the entity's assets were conveyed in its financial statements. To report on intention would be to forecast, and this is not the function of financial statements concerned with corresponding to what has happened to the business over a defined period of time. The use of sale prices in financial statements is an expression of the existing state of the entity's assets, and should not be taken as an implied statement that they are to be liquidated (although this may eventually happen in the normal course of business). Sale prices reflect potential not expected cash flows; they describe adaptability and command over resources, not liquidation proceeds.[31]

The specific asset classifications suggested for CFR reporting are as follows:

(1) realized assets (for example, cash and bank balances);

(2) readily-realizable assets (that is, those which have a ready market and sale price);
(3) not-readily-realizable assets (that is, those that do have a market and a sale price, but, which would not be readily or quickly realized because of the limited nature of the market); and
(4) not-realizable assets (that is, assets that have no market, and no known sale price; for this reason, they would be accounted for at a zero figure).

The complete asset structure would take the following simplified form:

	£
Realized assets	×
Readily-realizable assets	×
Not-readily-realizable assets	×
Not-realizable assets	×
	×

The report user thus would be provided with reasonably factual information on entity asset structure in terms of what has and could be generated in cash terms from assets held at the time of reporting. It would be described in accounting terms that are known and can be reasonably verified. If a sale price cannot be determined, this fact is readily admitted in the relevant statements by the appropriate classification. The structure is a means by which the report user can commence his assessment of the cash flow achievements and potential of the entity. In particular, it is attempting to account for the size and relative uncertainty of potential cash inflows held in the form of various assets existing at the time of reporting.

Liabilities of the entity also require to be classified – this time in terms of payability. They should be ordered from the immediately payable to those where repayment is indefinite. In this respect, the classifications necessary are reasonably identical to those used in conventional accounting practice, and do not require further explanation. This should not be surprising as such a classification is determined largely by legally enforceable contracts; a matter that is not altered by the particular method of accounting or reporting adopted. However, the payability classification is relevant to report users because of its potential to signal the size and timing of potential cash outflows as and when liabilities of the reporting entity fall due.

The classification and relating of the asset structure with its equivalent liability structure, both in terms of actual and potential cash flows, provide the means of producing four main financial statements reflecting the latter. These are explained in the following sections.

STATEMENT OF REALIZED CASH FLOW[32]

This statement reports on the actual cash inflow and outflows of the entity during a defined period. In particular, it is intended to provide the report user with a factual accounting of cash inflows from, for example, business operations (defined in terms of cash receipts from customers less cash payments to suppliers, employees and other providers of services needed in the trading activities of the entity); additional capital from the entity's owners (an occasional inflow in most cases); and additional short and long-term borrowing received. The major cash outflows would include cash payments for capital expenditure; taxation and distribution payments; and borrowing repayments. The outline of such a statement would be as follows (assuming net additional borrowing):

STATEMENT OF REALIZED CASH FLOW

	£
Cash inflows	
Operating cash flow	×
Additional borrowing	×
	×
Cash outflows	
Capital expenditure	×
Taxation paid	×
Distributions paid	×
	×

Several further points regarding presentation require to be made.

(1) Each of the separate datum in the above statement would require supporting notes to be disclosed, thereby providing needed detail as to its composition.
(2) Several of the figures are net aggregations, and deserve the additional disclosure advocated in (1).
(3) Individual aggregations may result in typical inflows being classified as outflows, and vice versa – for example, an operational cash flow deficit should appear as an outflow. Sale proceeds of fixed assets may exceed capital expenditure thus ensuring that the net figure should be treated as an inflow instead of the more typical outflow.
(4) Several periods' data will require reporting if an adequate view is to be given of the cash flow achievements of the entity. As will be explained in later chapters, a series of realized cash flows is useful for analysis purposes.

The Statement of Realized Cash Flow provides a report on the end-result of the financial management of the entity concerned. It describes where management has obtained cash required from, and the uses to which it has been put. In particular, it emphasizes the relative cash contributions from internal and external sources – the relationship, for example, between operating cash flow and additional borrowing. The statement also is intended to highlight the relative uses of available cash – especially between expenditure on capital items likely to provide operating cash flows in the future, and payments for tax and distributions for which nothing is received directly in return. Thus, the statement is clearly one in which report users ought to be able to discern the cash flow achievement of management and, particularly, to detect evidence of relative changes in input (internal v. external funding) and output (investment v. distribution).

STATEMENT OF REALIZABLE EARNINGS

The Statement of Realized Cash Flow describes only cash flows that have been achieved by the entity. It excludes those cash flows that are realizable, but remain unrealized, as the net assets concerned are in a non-cash form. The Statement of Realizable Earnings attempts to redress this omission by reporting on realized and unrealized cash flows. The combination of the two types of flow provides a measure of periodic profit equivalent to that derived in an SPA system. Realized cash flows already have been explained in the previous section in terms of operating cash flows, but unrealized cash flows deserve more explanation. They are a measure of the changes in the sale prices of all assets held during the period minus any periodic changes in the trading liabilities of the entity. Thus, they represent potential cash flow from net assets held by the latter for part or all of the period under consideration.

The production of the statement relies on an ordering of net assets in terms of realizability and payability. In this way, the realizable cash flows of the entity are disclosed according to how realizable they appear to be at the time of reporting. An outline statement is given below:

STATEMENT OF REALIZABLE EARNINGS

	£	£
Realized earnings		
Operating cash flow		×
Unrealized earnings		
Potential cash flows from:		
Readily-realizable net assets	×	
Not-readily-realizable net assets	×	×
Total realizable earnings		×
Less: taxation provided		×
		×
Less: distribution provided		×
		×
Add: retained earnings of prior periods		×
Retained earnings carried forward		×

Thus, the above statement provides a measure of periodic profit in sale price terms, utilizing the concept of cash flow. It distinguishes realized and unrealized elements of profit by introducing the principles of realizability and payability to cash flow classification. It further provides a measure of retained profit to be linked to the Statement of Financial Position. Other presentational points are as follows:

(1) As with the Statement of Realized Cash Flows, it is suggested that the Statement of Realizable Earnings be presented on a multi-period basis to provide a reasonable series of data. In particular, it would be important in this context to depict the relative contributions of realized and unrealized cash flows to total earnings, and any changes in such contributions – that is, to disclose the 'translation' of realizable net assets into cash resources. As stated before, it is only when such translations take place that profit figures have any financial signifiance from the point of view of funding such matters as investment and distributions.

(2) Whenever relevant, it would be desirable to support the aggregate data in the Statement of Realizable Earnings with annotated detail to provide report users with supplementary information.

(3) It is also possible to consider the maintenance of capital in generalized purchasing power terms – that is, to account for a necessary capital maintenance adjustment when there has been a general movement in price-levels such as to make the monetary measurement unit unstable over time.[33] The method suggested is the relatively simple one outlined by Chambers, in which the opening capital of the period is the basis for a single adjustment to periodic profit.[34] A relevant general price index movement is applied to the opening capital (including retained profit and other reserves), and the difference between the indexed and unadjusted capital figures is the amount by which the purchasing power of the opening capital has been eroded or enhanced. This amount is transferred from profit to a capital maintenance reserve (in the case of an inflation) or vice versa (in the case of a deflation). In order to keep subsequent discussions as simple as possible in this chapter, it will be assumed that the general price level is stable in all cases until page 71.

STATEMENT OF FINANCIAL POSITION

No system of financial reporting can be regarded as complete without a Statement of Financial Position that provides a report of the entity's financial position at the end of each defined operating period (that is, a balance sheet). The CFR system is no exception to this general rule, and it is advocated that such a statement should describe the cash flow potential of the entity in terms of its net assets disclosed in sale price terms – that is, in current cash equivalent terms. This would enable it to articulate with the previously mentioned Statements of Realized Cash Flow and Realizable Earnings. It would also indicate to report users the cash flow potential in the following accounting periods by adhering to the principles of realizability for assets and payability for liabilities. The structure of the Statement of Financial Position is outlined below:

STATEMENT OF FINANCIAL POSITION

	£	£
Realized assets		×
Readily-realized assets	×	
Less: short-term liabilities	×	×
Not-readily-realizable assets		×
Not-realizable assets		×
Total assets		×
Less: long-term liabilities		×
Total net assets		×
Owner's capital		×
Retained earnings		×
Owner's equity		×

The above Statement discloses to report users the net asset structure of the entity in order of realizability and in current sale price terms (assuming an orderly and usual realization).[35] It reveals how much of the asset structure is in the form of realized or readily-realizable assets, and how much represents assets that would be difficult or impossible to realize. It also informs the user about the funding of the entity, particularly regarding the timing of repayment of liabilities (even if only in general terms). As before, the disclosed figures ought to be supported, where relevant, with detailed notes and explanations, and the presentation ought to be a multiple-position one reflecting longer-term changes in the net asset structure and its parts, and compatible with the multi-period presentation in the Statements of Realized Cash Flows and Realizable Earnings.

STATEMENT OF CHANGES IN FINANCIAL POSITION

With the Statement of Financial Position providing an end-of period report of net assets and capital, it is clear that the other statements (of Realized Cash Flow and Realizable Earnings) do not inform the report user of all movements in financial position. However, they must inevitably capture some of the movements in order to reflect actual and potential cash flows of the period. The Statement of Realized Cash Flow discloses all completed cash flows, whether operational or otherwise, but reconciles to the periodic change in cash assets or borrowings. Similarly, the Statement of Realizable Earnings uses many of the cash flow movements but not all as it is concerned primarily with the movement in retained earnings. Thus, the Statement of Changes in Financial Position seeks to provide an overview of the changes in the financial position of the entity. These require to be drawn together into one statement that reconciles with the others but particularly with succeeding Statements of Financial Position. In a sense, it combines the movements described in the Statements of Realized Cash Flow and Realizable Earnings. As such, it amounts to a funds statement on a sale price basis, and is structured in outline as follows:

STATEMENT OF CHANGES IN FINANCIAL POSITION

	£	£
Realized cash inflow		
Increase in realized assets		×
Readily-realizable inflow		
Increase in readily-realizable assets	×	
Less: increase in short-term liabilities	×	×
Not-readily-realizable inflow		
Increase in not-readily-realizable assets		×
		×
Long-term cash outflow		
Increase in long-term liabilities		×
Indefinite cash outflow		
Retained earnings of the period		×
		×

As with the other statements, this statement utilizes the principles of asset realizability and liability payability. It would also require to disclose multi-period data to articulate with the other statements.

THE CFR SYSTEM

A quantified example of the four main financial statements advocated for a total CFR system hopefully will clarify the reporting structure. It follows the principles and practices outlined in the previous sections. The basic data from which the statements are derived are given as follows:

Assume the period of 1 January to 31 December, and the business of UV. At 1 January, he had the following assets and liabilities presented in the conventional form (all figures in £000s). Assets are described in sale price terms.

	£000	£000	£000
Fixed assets			
Property			12
Plant and machinery			9
Motor vehicles			10
			31
Current assets			
Stock of finished goods		10	
Work-in-progress		9	
Debtors		11	
Bank		5	
		35	
Less: current liabilities			
Creditors	9		
Taxation	13		
Distribution	10	32	3
			34
Equity			
Capital			10
Retained earnings			14
			24
Long-term liability			
Loan			10
			34

During the year to 31 December, the following transactions took place (all figures in £000s):

(1) Total sales on credit amounted to £194 and purchases of materials, wages and overheads on credit totalled £133.
(2) Work-in-progress costing £125 was transferred to finished goods stock, and the cost of finished goods sold was £119.
(3) Debtors paid £187 during the period, and £124 was paid to creditors. Other cash payments included £2 for interest, £13 for tax, £10 for distributions, and £7 for property. A long-term loan of £8 was received.
(4) The tax provision for the period was £20, and the distribution proposed at 31 December was £12.

At 31 December, the following sale prices pertained to the assets concerned: property £20; plant and machinery £6; motor vehicles £4; stock of finished goods £18; work-in-progress £24; and debtors £18. Creditors at the same date totalled £18, and the balance in the bank was £44.

From the above data, the following information and financial statements can be produced – in the form specified earlier and utilizing the principles of cash realizability and payability. But, first, the data require to be put in a state from which the required information can be accessed. This is done in the form of a worksheet and, in effect, summarizes the double-entry process that would be necessary to maintain the CFR system.

	Property	Plant and machinery	Motor vehicles	Finished goods	Work-in-progress	Debtors	Bank	Creditors	Taxation	Distributions	Loan	Capital	Retained earnings
	£000	£000	£000	£000	£000	£000	£000	£000	£000	£000	£000	£000	£000
Opening position	12	9	10	10	9	11	5	(9)	(13)	(10)	(10)	(10)	(14)
Credit sales						194							(194)
Cash from customers						(187)	187						
Credit purchases, wages, etc.					133			(133)					
Cash to suppliers, employees							(124)	124					
Cost of goods manufactured (a)				125	(125)								
Cost of goods sold (b)				(119)									119
Interest paid							(2)						2
Tax provided									(20)				20
Tax paid							(13)		13				
Distribution provided										(12)			12
Distribution paid							(10)			10			
Property purchased	7						(7)						
Loan received							8				(8)		
Sale price adjustments (c)	1	(3)	(6)	2	7								(1)
Closing position	20	6	4	18	24	18	44	(18)	(20)	(12)	(18)	(10)	(56)

From this schedule (which summarises the record-keeping function of the entity), it is now possible to produce the four required statements.

Statement of realized cash flow

As stated earlier, this statement describes the various cash inflows and outflows that have been achieved during the period concerned. These data are obtained in this case from the bank column in the worksheet.

STATEMENT OF REALIZED CASH FLOW
Year to 31 December

	Note	*£000*
Cash inflows		
Operating cash flow	1	61
Loan received		8
		69
Cash outflows		
Property purchased		7
Taxation paid		13
Distribution paid		10
Increase in cash asset	2	39
		69

Note		*£000*
1	Cash from customers	187
	Less: payments to suppliers, etc.	124
		63
	Less: interest paid	2
		61
2	Opening bank balance	5
	Less: closing bank balance	44
	Increase	39

Thus, it can be seen in this case and for this period that UV has generated most of his cash inflow from his trading operations and that, following tax and distribution payments, the majority of the available cash has increased his bank balance.

Statement of realizable earnings

The next statement reflects the profit of the period on a sale price basis but describing it in terms of realized and realizable cash flows. The information can be disclosed in one of the two ways. First, it can be derived from the retained earnings column of the worksheet.[36]

STATEMENT OF REALIZABLE EARNINGS (1)
Year to 31 December

	£000	*£000*
Sales		194
Less: cost of sales		119
		75
Less: interest		2
		73
Add: sale value adjustments:		
Property	1	
Plant and machinery	(3)	
Motor vehicles	(6)	
Finished goods	2	
Work-in-progress	7	1
		74
Less: taxation provided		20
		54
Less: distribution provided		12
		42
Add: retained earnings of prior periods		14
Retained earnings carried forward		56

Although this statement clearly provides information on the realizable earnings of UV, and articulates with the remainder of the data contained in the worksheet, it contains features that do not aid user comprehension of the cash flow situation of UV. First, it commences with a measure of historic cost-based profit (£73,000) that is dependent on cost allocation judgments in the measurement of stock and work-in-progress (and, thus, cost of sales); and, second, it contains measurements of sale price adjustments which are difficult to interpret – particularly in relation to stock and work-in-progress (gains of £2,000 and £7,000, respectively) where they are a mixture of a reversal of prior-period unrealized price changes now realized in the current period, and current period unrealized price changes.[37]

In order to avoid the need to disclose information depending on subjective cost allocations and difficult-to-interpret value adjustments, it is suggested that the Statement of Realizable Earnings should be prepared on a cash flow basis as follows:

STATEMENT OF REALIZABLE EARNINGS (2)
Year to 31 December

	£000	£000	£000
Realized earnings			
Operating cash flow (d)			61
Unrealized earnings			
Readily-realizable net assets:			
Debtors		7	
Stock of finished goods		8	
(Creditors)		(9)	
		6	
Motor vehicles		(6)	
Property (e)		1	
		1	
Not-readily-realizable net assets:			
Work-in-progress	15		
Plant and machinery	(3)	12	13
			74
Less: taxation provided			20
			54
Less: distribution provided			12
			42
Add: retained earnings of prior periods			14
Retained earnings carried forward			56

The raw data for this statement have been taken from the prepared worksheet. The operating cash flow data relate to operating activity and can be selected from the bank column. The remaining data are derived from an appropriate comparison of the opening and closing assets and liabilities relating to operating activity – that is, each of the asset categories minus the short-term trading liabilities represented by creditors. In this sense, the selection of data to prepare the statement is not as straightforward as for the first alternative statement.

Unrealized earnings constitute potential cash flows that have accrued during the period as a result of increases and decreases in the sale prices of assets, and net of periodic changes in trading liabilities. They therefore exclude either asset increases and decreases due to the purchase or sale of non-trading assets (in this case, an increase of £7,000 for property purchased) or changes in non-trading liabilities (in this case, an increase of £8,000 in long-term borrowing). Thus, the changes recorded represent potential cash inflows and outflows affecting the entity's reported earnings only.

The second Statement of Realizable Earnings provides the report user with a measure of the profitability of UV's business for the period, utilizing the cash flow concept and applying the principles of asset realizability and liability payability where relevant. It thereby articulates with each of the other statements in the CFR system. Realized earnings are represented by the operating cash flow of £61,000 (already described in the Statement of Realized Cash Flow). Unrealized earnings (£13,000) comprise the potential cash flows represented by the various periodic increases in net assets classified as readily-realizable (£1,000) and not-readily-realizable (£12,000). In other words, the pre-tax realizable profit of the period of £74,000 comprises £61,000 of realized cash, £1,000 of potentially readily-realizable cash and £12,000 of potentially not-readily-realizable cash (allowing for liabilities payable in the near future).

STATEMENT OF FINANCIAL POSITION
As at 31 December

	1 January £000	*31 December* £000
Cash assets		
Bank	5	44
Readily-realizable assets		
Debtors	11	18
Stock of finished goods	10	18
Motor vehicles	10	4
Property (f)	12	20
	43	60
Less: short-term liabilities		
Creditors	9	18
Taxation	13	20
Distribution	10	12
	32	50
	11	10
Not-readily-realizable assets		
Work-in-progress	9	24
Plant and machinery	9	6
	18	30
Net assets	34	84
Less: long-term liability		
Loans	10	18
	24	66
Owner's equity		
Capital	10	10
Retained earnings	14	56
	24	66

The statement of financial position

UV's financial position can be described in sale price terms both at the beginning and the end of the period. The figures required are derived easily from the worksheet as they represent the top and bottom lines of the latter.

This statement represents UV's balance sheet, and it articulates with the other statements in the CFR system. It is expressed in cash equivalent terms, and the assets and liabilities are ordered according to realizability and payability, respectively. By 31 December, UV has approximately one half of his net assets of £84,000 in the form of realized cash assets (£44,000). £10,000 is in the form of readily-realizable assets and a further £30,000 is not-readily-realizable. Long-term liabilities amount to £18,000 at the period-end. Thus, most of the net assets is in the form of realized or realizable cash flows and available to cover the long-term liability. In other words, even if not-readily-realizable cash flows are ignored, UV's business is very liquid and these readily-realizable funds are in excess of the original capital of £10,000.

Statement of changes in financial position

The Statement of Financial Position describes the entity's assets and liabilities at distinct points of time. A study of the comparative figures indicates movements in the individual items. Most of these have appeared in the Statement of Realized Cash Flow (if they concerned a cash transaction) and/or the Statement of Realizable Earnings (if they were related to the measurement of periodic profit). The Statement of Changes in Financial Position provides an opportunity to capture all actual and potential cash flow changes during the period within a single report. Using the data contained in the relevant worksheet, UV's Statement for the year to 31 December is as follows:

STATEMENT OF CHANGES IN FINANCIAL POSITION
Year to 31 December

	£000	£000	£000
Realized cash inflow			
Increase in bank balance			39
Unrealized cash inflow			
Readily-realized net assets:			
Debtors		7	
Stock of finished goods		8	
(Creditors)		(9)	
(Taxation provision)		(7)	
(Distribution provision)		(2)	
		(3)	
Motor vehicles		(6)	
Property		8	
		(1)	
Not-readily-realizable assets:			
Work-in-progress	15		
Plant and machinery	(3)	12	11
			50

Potential long-term cash outflow	
Additional loan	8
Potential indefinite cash outflow	
Retained earnings of period	42
	50

This is the total cash flow-based funds statement, measured by reference to the periodic movements on each of the stated balance sheet items (as seen in the worksheet, and also to be computed from the comparative figures in the Statement of Financial Position). In this case, it reveals £42,000 of total sale price-based funds generated in the form of retained profits, supplemented by a further £8,000 of borrowing – a total of £50,000 of additional funding, the substantial majority of which has been generated in the business. This has been matched by a corresponding increase of actual and potential cash inflow of £50,000 £39,000 of which is in the form of additional cash in the bank; a further increase of £12,000 is in a not-readily-realizable form; and there has been a decrease of £1,000 in readily-realizable net assets.

Each of the four main statements in the suggested CFR system has now been outlined. It is an articulating system of connected statements described in actual cash or potential cash terms (using sale prices for these latter measurements). It concentrates on the importance of cash flows to the business entity, and reflects the means by which net cash inflows are achieved – basically by the conversion of non-monetary assets into monetary assets (augmented by cash receipts from external sources). The vital importance of sale prices as means of describing such conversions ex ante is relatively obvious. In summary, therefore, the various statements describe the following cash flow features of the reporting entity:

(1) The Statement of Realized Cash Flow gives a complete overview of the total cash flow transactions during the defined period. The emphasis is on cash flow achievement rather than potential. It is essentially the financial statement that reflects the completion of the cash flow cycle; the conversion of non-cash assets into cash form; and, particularly, the cash contributions from operations. It is the fundamental statement of liquidity.

(2) The Statement of Realizable Earnings describes how better off the entity is in terms of an accounting for the conventional indicator of economic performance – periodic profit. In this instance, profit is disclosed in cash flow terms – that is, realized and unrealized cash flow. It is therefore the means by which the profit performance of the entity can be judged – not so much in terms of comparing sales and various costs (although this can be done), but in terms of actual and potential cash. In particular, it reveals how much of the periodic profit was available in cash form – an essential piece of information if the link between profitability and liquidity is accepted.

(3) The Statement of Financial Position is the 'stepping stone' report between cash flow statements, describing the net assets of the entity in

sale price terms thus providing information in aggregate form of the actual and potential cash available to the entity. This is essential information for those report users concerned with the realisability of the entity's assets.

(4) The Statement of Changes in Financial Position is the entity's funds statement expressed in terms of changes in the sale prices of net assets. It provides an explanation of all realized and potential cash flow changes for the period, including those affecting cash assets and retained earnings.

These explanations of the financial statements contained in the CFR system have dealt with the transactions of a single period. This has been necessary for purposes of simplifying the explanation. However, it should be reasonably clear that the cash flow cycles of individual entities may vary considerably depending on the nature of business concerned. Retail concerns will have a much shorter cycle than say manufacturing and contracting organizations. In order to reflect these cycles adequately, and to avoid the natural lumpiness of cash flows in individual periods, it is possible that the CFR system be regarded as a multi-period one rather than the conventional current-preceding year system of traditional accounting. Cash flow trends, successes, failures and problems are not matters in any case that appear suddenly. They are very much matters that grow over several periods, and signs of cash flow strengths and weaknesses require the examination of several periods' information. Whether this means multi-period reporting, or the accumulation of multi-period data by the report user, is a matter for serious debate. However, for purposes of this text, it is felt that multi-period reporting is preferable, and will be pursued further in this and later chapters. The following statements are offered in this respect – the overall period being five years, and the business being that of UV as throughout this chapter. The detailed workings are contained in Appendices 1 to 4.

STATEMENT OF REALIZED CASH FLOW
Year to 31 December

	1978 £000	*1979* £000	*1980* £000	*1981* £000	*1982* £000	*Total* £000
Cash inflows						
Operating cash flow*	61	71	57	50	46	285
Additional borrowing	8	—	—	—	4	12
Decrease in cash asset	—	15	—	15	18	48
	69	86	57	65	68	345
Cash outflows						
Capital expenditure	7	54	11	17	22	111
Taxation paid	13	20	17	18	16	84
Distribution paid	10	12	25	30	30	107
Increase in cash asset	39	—	4	—	—	43
	69	86	57	65	68	345

*	*1978* £000	*1979* £000	*1980* £000	*1981* £000	*1982* £000	*Total* £000
Cash from customers	187	210	232	238	261	1,128
Less: payments to suppliers, etc.	124	136	172	185	211	828
	63	74	60	53	50	300
Less: interest paid	2	3	3	3	4	15
Operating cash flow	61	71	57	50	46	285

STATEMENT OF REALIZABLE EARNINGS (1)
Year to 31 December

	1978 £000	*1979* £000	*1980* £000	*1981* £000	*1982* £000	*Total* £000
Sales	194	213	237	249	264	1,157
Less: cost of sales	119	128	166	179	200	792
	75	85	71	70	64	365
Less: interest	2	3	3	3	4	15
	73	82	68	67	60	350
Less: sale value adjustments:						
Property	(1)	(7)	(4)	(2)	(6)	(20)
Plant and machinery	3	18	13	14	9	57
Motor vehicles	6	7	6	6	7	32
Finished goods	(2)	(3)	—	(1)	—	(6)
Work-in-progress	(7)	1	1	3	2	—
	(1)	16	16	20	12	63
	74	66	52	47	48	287
Less: taxation provided	20	17	18	16	17	88
	54	49	34	31	31	199
Less: distribution provided	12	25	30	30	25	122
	42	24	4	1	6	77
Add: retained earnings of prior periods	14	56	80	84	85	14
Retained earnings carried forward	56	80	84	85	91	91

STATEMENT OF REALIZABLE EARNINGS (2)
Year to 31 December

	1978 *£000*	*1979* *£000*	*1980* *£000*	*1981* *£000*	*1982* *£000*	*Total* *£000*
Realized earnings						
Operating cash flow*	61	71	57	50	46	285
Unrealized earnings						
Readily-realizable net assets:						
Debtors	7	3	5	11	3	29
Stock of finished goods	8	7	5	5	5	30
(Creditors)	(9)	(1)	(8)	—	(3)	(21)
	6	9	2	16	5	38
Motor vehicles	(6)	(7)	(6)	(6)	(7)	(32)
Property	1	7	4	2	6	20
	1	9	—	12	4	26
Not-readily-realizable assets:						
Work-in-progress	15	4	8	(1)	7	33
Plant and machinery	(3)	(18)	(13)	(14)	(9)	(57)
	12	(14)	(5)	(15)	(2)	(24)
	74	66	52	47	48	287
Less: taxation provided	20	17	18	16	17	88
	54	49	34	31	31	199
Less: distribution provided	12	25	30	30	25	122
	42	24	4	1	6	77
Less: retained earnings of prior periods	14	56	80	84	85	14
Retained earnings carried forward	56	80	84	85	91	91

*	*1978* *£000*	*1979* *£000*	*1980* *£000*	*1981* *£000*	*1982* *£000*	*Total* *£000*
Cash from customers	187	210	232	238	261	1,128
Less: payments to suppliers, etc.	124	136	172	185	211	828
	63	74	60	53	50	300
Less: interest paid	2	3	3	3	4	15
Operating cash flow	61	71	57	50	46	285

STATEMENT OF FINANCIAL POSITION
As at 31 December

	1977 £000	*1978* £000	*1979* £000	*1980* £000	*1981* £000	*1982* £000
Cash asset						
Bank	5	44	29	33	18	—
Readily-realizable assets						
Debtors	11	18	21	26	37	40
Stock of finished goods	10	18	25	30	35	40
Motor vehicles	10	4	17	11	5	13
Property	12	20	27	31	33	39
	43	60	90	98	110	132
Less: short-term liabilities						
Creditors	9	18	19	27	27	30
Taxation	13	20	17	18	16	17
Distribution	10	12	25	30	30	25
	32	50	61	75	73	72
	11	10	29	23	37	60
Not-readily-realizable assets						
Work-in-progress	9	24	28	36	35	42
Plant and machinery	9	6	22	20	23	21
	18	30	50	56	58	63
Net assets	34	84	108	112	113	123
Less: long-term liability						
Loans	10	18	18	18	18	22
	24	66	90	94	95	101
Owner's equity						
Capital	10	10	10	10	10	10
Retained earnings	14	56	80	84	85	91
	24	66	90	94	95	101

STATEMENT OF CHANGES IN FINANCIAL POSITION
Year to 31 December

	1978 £000	1979 £000	1980 £000	1981 £000	1982 £000	Total £000
Realized cash inflow						
Increase in cash asset	39	(15)	4	(15)	(18)	(5)
Unrealized cash inflow						
Readily-realized net assets:						
Debtors	7	3	5	11	3	29
Stock of finished goods	8	7	5	5	5	30
(Creditors)	(9)	(1)	(8)	—	(3)	(21)
(Taxation provision)	(7)	3	(1)	2	(1)	(4)
(Distribution provision)	(2)	(13)	(5)	—	5	(15)
	(3)	(1)	(4)	18	9	19
Motor vehicles	(6)	13	(6)	(6)	8	19
Property	8	7	4	2	6	27
	(1)	19	(6)	14	23	49
Not-readily-realizable assets:						
Work-in-progress	15	4	8	(1)	7	33
Plant and machinery	(3)	16	(2)	3	(2)	12
	12	20	6	2	5	45
	11	39	—	16	28	94
	50	24	4	1	10	89
Potential long-term cash outflow						
Additional loan	8	—	—	—	4	12
Potential indefinite cash outflow						
Retained earnings of period	42	24	4	1	6	77
	50	24	4	1	10	89

The reporting of five years of cash flow-based data provides the report user with a means of judging the profitability and liquidity of this manufacturing business over a reasonable period, and avoiding possible misconceptions of its cash flow problems caused by examining too short a period. Chapter 7 will describe the process of CFR-based financial analysis in more detail but, meantime, the following general points are reasonably clear from the above financial statements (the detailed data on which the latter have been based are contained on pages 66–67 and in Appendices 1 to 4).

(1) From the Statement of Realized Cash Flow, it can be seen that much of the cash flow input over the five-year period has come from operations. The majority of cash outflow has taken the form of tax and distribution payments, although the single largest outflow relates to capital expenditure.
(2) The first Statement of Realizable Earnings is given for information

only in order to provide a record of historic cost-based profits for purposes which require such measurements (for example, taxation).

(3) The second Statement of Realizable Earnings reveals that realized cash flows have been augmented by readily-realizable price changes, and diminished by not-readily-realizable changes. The overall result, however, is that pre-tax realizable profits are comprised largely of realized cash flows.

(4) The balance sheet situation is described in the five-year Statement of Financial Position. In this, it is possible to detect the decline in cash assets and the increase in readily-realizable net assets and not-readily-realizable assets. By the end of the five-year period, the position is one in which the total net assets are divided approximately equally between the latter two categories – that is, the business has had consistently about one-half of its net resources in a not-readily-realizable form.

(5) The changes commented on in outline in (4) are more clearly evidenced in the Statement of Changes in Financial Position. The decline in cash assets, the increase in readily-realizable net assets, and the much greater increase in not-readily-realizable assets, are matters that the analyst would require to investigate further (and this will be done in Chapter 7).

(6) As stated earlier in the chapter, the question of capital maintenance in situations of general price instability has to be considered. The capital maintenance adjustment recommended is a single one based on opening capital figures. In this case, the index movements are as follows (each index point is taken at the relevant period-end): 1977 100; 1978 110; 1979 121; 1980 133; 1981 146; and 1982 161.

Using the above data, the Statements of Realizable Earnings and Financial Position appear as follows:

STATEMENT OF MAINTAINED REALIZABLE EARNINGS
Year to 31 December

	1978 £000	1979 £000	1980 £000	1981 £000	1982 £000	Total £000
Total earnings before distribution	54	49	34	31	31	199
Less: capital maintenance adjustment (g)	2	7	9	9	10	37
	52	42	25	22	21	162
Less: distribution provided	12	25	30	30	25	122
	40	17	(5)	(8)	(4)	40
Add: retained earnings of prior periods	14	54	71	66	58	14
Retained earnings carried forward	54	71	66	58	54	54

STATEMENT OF MAINTAINED FINANCIAL POSITION
At 31 December

	1978	*1979*	*1980*	*1981*	*1982*
	£000	*£000*	*£000*	*£000*	*£000*
Capital	10	10	10	10	10
Capital maintenance reserve (h)	2	9	18	27	37
Retained earnings (i)	54	71	66	58	54
	66	90	94	95	101

The above figures reveal the impact of an approximate and compounding inflation of 10% on total realizable earnings. Only in 1978 and 1979 are earnings sufficient both to maintain the purchasing power of opening capital and cover the distributions provided. In the remaining years, maintenance of capital in purchasing power terms has revealed the over-distribution of real earnings. This is summarized clearly in the Statement of Maintained Financial Position in which retained earnings are diminishing at the same time as the capital maintenance reserve is increasing.

This is obviously a vital issue when considering the financial performance of the reporting entity generally and, more specifically, when the suitability of its distribution policy is considered. However, for purposes of concentrating attention on other issues, general price-level stability will be assumed in Chapter 6 onwards.

CHAPTER 6 Arguments for a CFR system

INTRODUCTION

The previous chapter aims at familiarizing the reader with the suggested CFR system. It is now appropriate to present the various arguments that can be made for it. They are each regarded as of equal importance and will be related, where relevant, to the accounting data and financial statements utilized in the previous chapter. Before proceeding to the detail of these arguments, however, the reader should be reminded that the latter are not presented as a means of countering the cases to be made for reporting systems such as historic cost accounting and replacement cost accounting. There are no doubt arguments to be made for non-cash flow systems. But this text is aimed at prescribing CFR as a system that is required by several report-user groups for specific reasons. These reasons will be explained fully in this chapter.

PROFITS AND CASH FLOW

As the examples in the previous chapter explain, CFR is a system of reporting that combines cash flows and sale prices. It therefore has the unique benefit to the report user of reporting on both profitability and liquidity. The essential feature is cash flow, and the main message is how much of that cash flow is derived from available profits. For example, taking the five years of reported cash flow results of UV, the following cash flow–profit relationships are evident:

CASH FLOWS AND HISTORIC COST PROFITS
Year to 31 December

	1978 *£000*	*1979* *£000*	*1980* *£000*	*1981* *£000*	*1982* *£000*	*Total* *£000*
Historic cost profit before tax (a)	73	82	68	67	60	350
Operating cash flow (b)	61	71	57	50	46	285
Difference increase in working capital (c)	12	11	11	17	14	65

What this comparison reveals is that in each year, the realized profit has not been available fully in cash due to the continuous build up of working capital. In fact, over the five year period, 81% of realized profit before depreciation has been translated into operating cash flow (£285,000/350,000). However, subjective judgments are contained in the realized profit figures (particularly due to the cost allocations required for stock purposes), thus an alternative comparison of profits and cash flows could be given which avoids these judgments – that is, by comparing in the same cash or cash-equivalent terms:

CASH FLOWS AND REALIZABLE PROFITS
Year to 31 December

	1978	*1979*	*1980*	*1981*	*1982*	*Total*
	£000	*£000*	*£000*	*£000*	*£000*	*£000*
Realizable earnings before tax (d)	74	66	52	47	48	287
Operating cash flow (d)	61	71	57	50	46	285
Difference = unrealized cash flows	13	(5)	(5)	(3)	2	2

Thus, by introducing sale prices and unrealized gains and losses, it is possible to disclose in this particular case that the total realizable profits of UV have been almost entirely matched by realized operating cash flows; and that the small differences comprise much larger but compensating movements in the sale prices of net assets being held throughout the periods concerned. Potential cash flow increases in this case (for example, over the five years, £38,000 for readily-realizable working capital, £20,000 for property, and £33,000 for work-in-progress) have been reasonably matched by potential cash flow decreases (£32,000 for motor vehicles and £57,000 for plant)[d]. It would therefore appear that long-term operating cash flows are reasonable surrogates for realisable profits in this case.

IMPORTANCE OF USERS

As with all financial reporting systems, the argument for CFR must contain reference to the importance of user needs. They remain as a key feature of any system – without them, there appears little point in producing and reporting accounting information; with them, there appears every need to examine closely precise informational requirements. CFR is no exception to this point and, from such an examination, the role of the system can be appreciated.

The major report user groups have been identified in Chapter 4 as owners, lenders (including bankers), suppliers, customers, employees and government. Each such group has its own specific interest in the reporting entity – for example, owners are concerned with distributions; lenders and bankers with borrowing repayments; suppliers with debt repayments; customers with continuity of business; employees with wages levels; and government with tax liabilities. Each of these groups will be examined in the context of UV's business in order to provide a basis from which general points can be made concerning the CFR system.

CFR AND OWNERS

The owner is UV. He has an original investment of £10,000. The CFR system provides him with information of potential relevance as follows – he has received total distributions of £107,000 over the five-year period.[c]; and at the same time, his equity stake has increased in realisable terms from £24,000 to £101,000; that is, by £77,000[f]:

	£	£
Increase in readily-realizable net assets (g)		49,000
Increase in not-readily-realizable net assets (h)		45,000
		94,000
Less: decrease in cash assets (i)	5,000	
increase in long-term loans (j)	12,000	17,000
		77,000

Thus, most of the equity increase is in a readily-realizable form providing UV with a potential adaptability considerably greater than at the beginning of the five-year period (that is, an ability to change the nature of his business and/or its operations). In fact, such a development has been a continuous affair in each year. However, of the total net assets of £24,000 at 31 December 1977, £16,000 (67%) was in cash or potentially near-cash form (realized assets £5,000 and readily-realizable net assets £11,000). But, by the end of 1982, the equivalent datum was 49% (none of which was in realized form)[k]. Therefore, although UV appears to have a greater potential adaptability by 1982, his net asset structure is marginally less realizable than in 1977.

Little of this information would have been forthcoming in conventional accounting, other than that concerning distributions. CFR provides owners with an in-depth disclosure of entity profits and cash flows. UV's command over resources (that is, his ability to acquire resources measured in terms of sale prices or current cash equivalents) has been described fully, particularly with regard to realizability. The entity's profits have also been portrayed in terms of cash flows, again with the emphasis on realizability. Between 31 December 1977 and 31 December 1982, UV's command over resources has increased considerably, despite significant distributions, but at the cost of decreasing net asset realizability.

CFR AND LENDERS

The entity's lenders and bankers would benefit from receipt of its CFR information. They are concerned essentially with cash flow and liquidity, and CFR is a system which appears to be constructed specifically to meet their needs. In the case of UV, the relevant information is as follows.

First, the entity has relied little on external funding. During the five-year period (see Statement of Realized Cash Flow), operating cash flows of

£285,000 amounted to 83% of the total cash inflow of £345,000. A further £12,000 was borrowed long-term, and the remaining £5,000 came from an existing bank balance. However, the trend of operating cash flow has been falling and, by 31 December 1982, all existing cash assets have been consumed. Thus, it would appear that, if outflows are to continue at 1982 levels or more, further borrowing may be necessary – for example, from the bank. In addition, the relative lowness of capital expenditure compared with other outflows such as tax and distributions is a factor to be considered seriously. Over five years, expenditure totalled £302,000[l], of which £111,000 (37%) was spent on capital expenditure; £84,000 (28%) on taxation; and £107,000 (35%) on distributions. A low level of capital expenditure, particularly in a manufacturing entity over a long period of time, may warn lenders and bankers of poor operating cash flow returns to come, more borrowing, and less available to repay the latter eventually.

Second, the financial position of the entity (see Statement of Financial Position), when expressed in sale price terms, indicates the degree of available security to a lender or banker. In the case of UV's business, the long-term loan of £10,000 at 31 December 1977 was covered by realizable net assets of £34,000, of which £16,000 (47%) was in realized or near-cash form. In other words, the debt could be secured adequately by the realizable net assets (cover 1.6[m] ignoring not-readily-realizable assets). By 31 December 1982, however, long-term borrowing had grown to £22,000. Available net assets of £123,000 covered this, but £63,000 (51%) was in the form of not-readily-realizable assets, and none of the cover was in the form of cash assets. Thus, the lender would see from these CFR statements that the realizable net asset cover had been maintained over the five-year period, but at a loss of available realized assets owing to the erosion of cash assets.

Lender and banker would therefore be given information relating to the conversion of profits into cash flow; the degree to which available cash is used for reinvestment and distribution; and the realizable asset cover for borrowings. Such information would not be available easily or directly in the conventional allocation-based accounting systems.

CFR AND SUPPLIERS

The suppliers to UV's business would have similar information needs to those of its lender and banker – albeit the time horizon of the latter persons may be somewhat longer. Conventional accounting disclosures would enable suppliers to examine the repayment record of the business in terms of creditors turnover ratios (taken as cost of sales related to average creditors, and converted to number of days credit[n]:

Year	(1) *Average creditors* £000	(2) *Cost of sales* £000	(3) *Factor* (2) ÷ (1)	(4) *Credit (days)* 365 ÷ (3)
1978	13.5	119	8.8	41
1979	18.5	128	6.9	53
1980	23.0	166	7.2	51
1981	27.0	179	6.6	55
1982	28.5	200	7.0	52

Thus, on average, credit of approximately 50 days was given by suppliers. This would appear to indicate a stability in collection and repayment. The Statement of Realized Cash Flow reveals the ability of the entity to meet its obligations in this respect – each year producing an operating cash flow surplus following payments due to suppliers. This stability is more clearly seen when comparing total credit purchases of materials, wages and overheads in each year with the equivalent cash payments:

	1978 *£000*	*1979* *£000*	*1980* *£000*	*1981* *£000*	*1982* *£000*	*Total* *£000*
Total credit purchases (1)	133	137	180	185	214	849
Cash payments to suppliers (2)	124	136	172	185	211	828
Percentage payment: (2) ÷ (1)	93%	99%	96%	100%	99%	98%

With the exception of 1978, nearly all credit purchases were paid in the period concerned. The overall difference of £21,000 accounts for the increase in creditors from £9,000 at 31 December 1978 to £30,000 at 31 December 1982.

In addition, at the end of each year, suppliers would be informed by a sale price-based Statement of Financial Position of the cover available for the business' debt to them:

	1977 *£000*	*1978* *£000*	*1979* *£000*	*1980* *£000*	*1981* *£000*	*1982* *£000*
Cash asset	5	44	29	33	18	—
Readily-realized assets	43	60	90	98	110	132
	48	104	119	131	128	132
Less: taxation (o)	13	20	17	18	16	17
Available cover	35	84	102	113	112	115
Creditors	9	18	19	27	27	30
Times covered	3.9	4.7	5.4	4.2	4.2	3.8

Realizable cover therefore increased through 1977 to 1979, and has dropped somewhat since then (but not disastrously). The main problem appears to be the lack of realized assets, as the bank balance was reduced to nil by 1982.

CFR AND CUSTOMERS

Customers, too, have an interest in the financial results of a business. They are concerned with continuity of service as well as with the terms of credit provided by it. In the case of UV, his customers would see from the Statement of Realized Cash Flow that the business appeared to have been financially viable throughout the five-year period. They also could determine from a study of the Statements of Realized Cash Flow and Realizable Earnings that most of the sales recognized during the period had been collected in cash:

	1978	*1979*	*1980*	*1981*	*1982*	*Total*
	£000	*£000*	*£000*	*£000*	*£000*	*£000*
Total credit sales (1)	194	213	237	249	264	1,157
Cash from customers (2)	187	210	232	238	261	1,128
Percentage collection: (2) ÷ (1)	96%	99%	98%	96%	99%	97%

There therefore appears to have been a consistent collection of debt by the business, and this is obviously beneficial to its long-term liquidity situation. However, this is only one part of the story – the 1%, 2%, 3% or 4% lack of collection of cash merely increases the level of debtors and, in this case, they are increasing at a faster pace than sales (by 264%[p] between 1977 and 1982 compared with the equivalent sales statistic of 36%[q]). This can be verified by examining the number of days of credit given to customers (a matter that can be obtained from CFR and conventional accounting systems):

	1978	*1979*	*1980*	*1981*	*1982*
	£000	*£000*	*£000*	*£000*	*£000*
Total sales (1)	194	213	237	249	264
Average debtors (2)	14.5	19.5	23.5	31.5	38.5
Credit factor (3): (1) ÷ (2)	13.4	10.9	10.1	7.9	6.9
Credit (days): 365 ÷ (3)	27	33	36	46	53

Thus, it can be seen that the business is, on average, providing more credit for its customers year by year (by 1982, almost twice the 1978 period of credit). These findings would give cause for concern when taken in conjunction with the previous ones. Increasing credit terms may appear beneficial to customers, but it is not so helpful to the business as it delays the receipt of needed cash. With the earlier cash analysis revealing that, in terms of actual cash received in each period, an average of 97% of the sales of the period had been collected, it is clear that increasing sales were not being recovered fully. In other words, the average extending of customer credit had not increased the total cash inflow from customers at the same pace as the increasing sales. Under these circumstances, it must be argued that the CFR system provides customers (and other report users) with additional information regarding the business' policy and practice regarding customers, and the impact of these matters on its cash flow.

CFR AND EMPLOYEES

One of the most important groups of constituents in any business in that of employees, and the business of UV is no exception. His employees presumably would be much concerned with matters such as job prospects, wages levels and job conditions. The CFR-based information would be relevant to these needs. First, the complete package of financial information reveals that, over the last five years, the business has been both profitable and liquid. The operating cash flows have been diminishing but remain by far the largest single contribution to the cash funding of the business.

The figures for realizable earnings also provide a means of explaining its profitability in terms of cash flows which, arguably, is a more realistic way of viewing funds available for meeting wage claims and additional employee benefits. Too often, in wage and related negotiations, profits are attributed wrongly with cash flow meanings. Only when they are described in the latter terms, as in the CFR system, will this type of identification be legitimate.

In the case of UV, total retained profits (after tax and distribution) have been as follows (as per the Statement of Realizable Earnings):

	1978	*1979*	*1980*	*1981*	*1982*	*Total*
	£000	*£000*	*£000*	*£000*	*£000*	*£000*
Retained earnings	42	24	4	1	6	77

Thus, it may be assumed by employees that the business has accumulated £77,000 of funds 'surplus to requirements'. However, as the Statement of Changes in Financial Position reveals, this increase has been matched by corresponding changes in other items:

	£000	*£000*
Increase in realizable value of:		
Readily-realizable net assets		49
Not-readily-realizable assets		45
		94
Less: additional long-term borrowing	12	
consumption of cash asset	5	17
		77

The retained earnings have therefore been re-invested in the net assets of the business – none are in realized form, and almost one-half are not-readily-realizable (being in the form of work-in-progress and plant and machinery). The profits of the business have funded its development, and have been committed to specific resources.

This can be more clearly seen in an alternative way in the Statement of Realized Cash Flow (taking the five-year total figures):

	£000	%
Cash inflows		
Operating cash flow	285	94
Additional borrowing	12	4
Decrease in cash asset (r)	5	2
	302	100
Cash outflows		
Capital expenditure	111	37
Taxation paid	84	28
Distributions paid	107	35
	302	100

With the translation of profits into operating cash flows, the latter have been utilized on capital expenditure, tax and distributions. But what may concern employees in this respect is the comparison of capital expenditure with distributions. There may well be reasonable explanations for equivalence of the two items in this case, but a lack of investment can affect job prospects, and the future of the business can be jeopardized by excessive distributions.

CFR AND GOVERNMENT

The major government agency concerned to receive financial information about UV's business would be the tax authorities. In this case, their main interest would be in the entity's historic cost profits, stock levels and capital expenditure:

	1978 £000	*1979* £000	*1980* £000	*1981* £000	*1982* £000
Historic cost profits before depreciation	73	82	68	67	60
End-of-period stock and work-in-progress	29	38	52	58	72
Capital expenditure:					
Property	7	—	—	—	—
Plant and machinery	—	34	11	17	7
Motor vehicles	—	20	—	—	15
	7	54	11	17	22

Each of the above datum is expressed in historic cost terms, and is required for purposes of computing the business' tax liabilities – the basis is historic cost profit (subject to various legally prescribed adjustments where necessary); the appropriateness of the computation of stock and work-in-progress would be examined in detail, and capital expenditure would be analysed to assess its suitability as a deductible item. The capital expenditure would be available in the CFR system, as would historic cost profits (if the Statements of Realized Earnings contained these data). But historic cost stock and work-in-progress would not be reported under CFR, and would require to be supplied separately to the tax authorities.

Thus, the CFR system does not appear to be suited specifically to the needs of the latter. It does, however, provide other report users with data regarding the entity's ability to pay tax. First, the Statement of Realized Cash Flow reveals in the case of UV adequate cash funds to meet the taxation liabilities when due:

	1978	*1979*	*1980*	*1981*	*1982*	*Total*
	£000	*£000*	*£000*	*£000*	*£000*	*£000*
Operating cash flow (1)	61	71	57	50	46	285
Taxation paid (s) (2)	13	20	17	18	16	84
Cash flow cover (1) ÷ (2)	4.7	3.6	3.4	2.8	2.9	3.4

The above figures reveal that the operating cash flow cover has been diminishing over the five-year period, as lower operating surpluses cover tax payments based on higher levels of profits in the previous periods. The cover has dropped from nearly 5 times in 1978 to approximately 3 times in 1982. Thus, there is little cause for concern regarding the availability of cash to meet tax demands in the last five years, but the position in this respect is deteriorating.

Second, report users could examine the impact of its tax policies on business, not in terms of profits but in cash flow terms – that is, using the CFR information to measure the cash flow-based tax effect (figures taken from the Statement of Realized Cash Flow):

	1978	*1979*	*1980*	*1981*	*1982*	*Total*
	£000	*£000*	*£000*	*£000*	*£000*	*£000*
Operating cash flow	61	71	57	50	46	285
Less: capital expenditure (t)	7	54	11	17	22	111
Taxable cash flow (1)	54	17	46	33	24	174
Taxation paid (2)	13	20	17	18	16	84
Cash flow tax rate (%) [(2) ÷ (1) × 100]	24	118	37	55	67	48

The tax rate applied in each of the five years to UV's business historic cost-based profits was 30%. Yet, when disregarding this and substituting a cash flow basis, the rate varies considerably – from 24% to 118%, and averaging 48%. This is considerably greater than the prescribed rate, and indicates the tax burden in cash terms which this business is bearing.

GENERAL POINTS CONCERNING UTILITY

Several general points concerning the utility of the CFR system can be made from the above analyses of individual report user groups.

(1) All groups are concerned essentially with matters relating to the future. Ideally, this is what they require information about in terms of their differing decision models. Owners search for indicators of future distributions; lenders, bankers and suppliers are interested in future repayments; customers are concerned with the future supply of goods and services; employees need information about job prospects; and government (in the form of the tax authorities) has to assess a liability to tax that will be payable in the future. But the CFR system as described in this text is limited to an accounting and disclosure of past information. Nevertheless, it has been argued in the previous sections that utility exists in CFR. For example:

   (i) For owners, the entity's distribution record is disclosed in terms of both profits realized, and cash flows available to cover such outflows. Both matters are key factors in decisions concerned with cash distributions.
   (ii) For lenders, bankers and suppliers, the past record of repayment is disclosed in detail – that is, whether or not the entity was able to make cash repayments when due.
   (iii) For customers, the past profitability and liquidity of the entity are described fully, providing information on its ability to survive and to continue to provide a service.
   (iv) For employees, CFR not only describes the profit and cash flow record of the entity but also provides information on cash generated from profits and the uses to which such cash has been put.

   What the CFR system does not do is make a value judgment as to the chances of the entity's past cash flow record or trend being continued in the future. Such predictions are regarded in this text as matters for the judgment of the user rather than the producer of financial statements. What CFR provides is a factual basis from which such judgments can be made by the user.

(2) All groups appear to have an interest in cash flow, and a consequent need for information describing it. CFR caters for this general need and does so in a way that attempts to be helpful to the individual user – that is, by describing the entity's assets and liabilities in cash or cash equivalent terms using sale prices, and thereby giving factual descriptions from which insights to future cash inflows and outflows can be made by the user. Assets and liabilities described in terms of current cash equivalents provide a foundation for user predictions of cash flows in a reasonably objective way using market prices when these are available.

(3) The description of the net asset structure of the entity in sale price terms provides the financial reporter with the opportunity of

supplying all report-user groups with reasonably factual information concerning the translation of assets into cash inflows, the extinguishing of liabilities by cash outflows, cash inflows which create further liabilities, and the translation of cash back into non-monetary assets. This constant cycle of transactions, completed in cash terms, gives users a basis for judging the cash flow potential of the entity, and it is the latter that provides ultimately the various returns to interested report-user groups.

(4) The reporting of net assets in cash terms, as well as the intervening cash flows, has the additional benefit to report users of causing reporting accountants to consider the classification of assets and liabilities, and cash inflows and outflows. In particular, accounting classifications must be made in CFR in order to determine the realizability of assets, the payability of liabilities, and whether surpluses and deficits are realized or realizable. Users are therefore given some idea of the uncertainties associated with cash generation in the past, which must be of some benefit from the point of view of prediction. This is a much neglected area by accountants, and the traditional classifications do not appear to be suitable if adequate cash flow information is to be provided.

SPECIFIC POINTS OF UTILITY

The above general points have been given as supports to the main thesis of this text that CFR is beneficial to users in a general way – that is, it is not directed at one specific group to the exclusion of others because it is a system of reporting that does not exclude users – its universality is such that all users must benefit because of the fundamental nature of cash flow in business and its relationship to their various decision models. With this in mind, it appears appropriate to elaborate on the specific points of utility which bring this condition of universality to CFR.

FINANCIAL VIABILITY AND SURVIVAL

The most basic financial point to be made about any business is one that was elaborated in the introduction to this text – without cash flow, the business entity cannot survive. Survival is therefore conditional on the receipt of cash sufficient to meet the cash payments due by the entity. This is such a common-sense point that it appears almost trivial to make it. Surprisingly, it may well be a message that is lost on many businessmen and managers who believe wrongly that profitability is the sole means of survival in business, and that continuing cash shortages can be compensated by borrowing.

CFR is a system of accounting and reporting that corrects these false notions. It provides crucial information on the availability of cash from profitable operations; the relative reliance for cash funding from the latter internal source and external sources such as bank borrowings; and the use of available cash for investment and distribution purposes. Because cash flows usually mark the completion of one transaction and the beginning of the next, their reporting is a reasonably factual means of disclosing arguably the most fundamental financial issues facing the business. No matter how profitable it is, cash flows must be provided from profits as soon as possible if the entity is to survive. Financial viability and survival are long-term matters. CFR provides relevant information reflecting long-term viability and survival. A simple example serves to illustrate these points.

WX enters into an agreement with a supplier to buy goods on credit for £120. He then enters into a further agreement with a customer to sell these goods on credit to the latter person for £160. So far, no cash transactions have taken place as the buying and selling of goods have been on credit. Both transactions are therefore incomplete. The realized profit on sale, however, is £40[u], and the balance sheet picture would be as follows:

	£
Debtor	160
Less: creditor	120
	40
Retained profit	40

The importance of cash and cash flow to WX and his business now become apparent. He may have 'realized' a profit of £40, but he cannot enjoy it by way of distribution unless cash is also available. His creditor cannot be repaid for the same reason. Thus, completion of the sale transaction by receipt of the cash due by the debtor of £160 is necessary and this would, in turn, enable completion of the purchase transaction by payment of the £120 due, leaving £40 of cash available to WX to decide whether to consume or retain (ignoring the question of taxation).

But suppose WX has borrowed £20 from a bank, ostensibly to pay for stock but in reality to pay for a distribution of profit of the same amount. His amended balance sheet position would be as follows:

	£	£
Debtor		160
Less: creditor	120	
bank overdraft	20	140
		20
Retained profit (v)		20

This admittedly over-simplified situation reveals the seeds of business failure – profitability without cash flow, leading to borrowing in order to enable the distribution to be made. WX may have benefited in the short-term from his £20 distribution. But the bank and the creditor are both in danger of losing their 'investment' unless the debtor meets his obligation, and the probability of this happening may be partly a function of how efficient WX is as a financial manager. Beyond the short-term, he is likely to fail so long as cash inflows are inadequate in relation to the cash outflow needs of the business. In this case, WX, the bank and the supplier will all lose unless cash comes in from the customer.

A CFR system of reporting would aid the identification of these problems for WX and others concerned about his business – that is, a Statement of Realized Cash Flow, particularly, would reveal bank borrowings of £20 to fund the cash distribution of the same amount, and no operating cash flow. The Statement of Financial Position would reveal (as above) the dependence of the bank and the supplier on the customer's ability to pay debts when due.

CASH GENERATION

If the needs of all the report user groups were to be reduced to a single factor it would be cash flow returns. Nearly all users are interested in the returns to be made to them by the entity, and these are made normally in cash flow terms. Thus, owners look for distributions; lenders, bankers and suppliers expect repayments (including interest where relevant); employees receive wages for their services; and the tax authorities are entitled legally to tax revenues due.

The question of cash flow returns is therefore a key issue for these groups. In turn, the cash flow generating potential of the entity must be of considerable interest. Unless it can generate cash to provide adequate returns to interested parties, they will not receive what is due to them in terms either of contracts and/or the risks they have taken. Many accounting studies and pronouncements have agreed and accepted this point.[38] But they have proceeded to suggest or prescribe systems of accounting and reporting that fail to report on the cash generation of the entity. Instead, systems that obscure underlying cash flows are the usual feature.[39] CFR attempts to reveal not just the cash flows realized by the entity but also those that are realizable. Users interested in cash returns cannot argue that CFA ignores their needs in this respect.

The situation of WX can be used to demonstrate user interest in the cash-generating ability of a business.

Assuming the balance sheet situation described above, it is clear that the supplier (£120 owed) and the bank (£20 owed) would be concerned with the generation of cash from the customer (£160 due). The latter debt may be readily-realizable, but much depends on the extent to which cash is forthcoming. There are a range of possibilities:

(1) The debt is irrecoverable, in which case the supplier and the banker will not be repaid by the business without a personal guarantee by WX or a court case.
(2) The debt is partly recoverable. Anything less than an 87.5% recovery

(£140) would mean either the supplier or the bank (or both) would not recover the full amount of the debt owed to them.

(3) The debt is fully or more than 87.5% recovered. In this case, the liabilities would be repaid, and any remaining cash would be available to WX for various purposes (including reinvestment in stock and/or further distribution).

Thus, WX would also be concerned about the cash-generating potential of his business – recovery of the figure of £160 would enable him to meet his obligations and remain better off by £20. The CFR system of accounting would provide all persons concerned with information on this facet of WX's financial affairs. In particular, the Statement of Financial Position would reveal the dependence of the supplier and the bank on the recovery of the readily-realizable debt (which should be reported at its expected recoverable amount).[40]

COMMAND OVER RESOURCES

As with Man and animals, businesses survive in the long-run by adaptation – that is, they develop and change according to the conditions and environment which influence them. Businesses are subject to changing consumer demands and tastes, technological developments, additional legal and social constraints, different economic market conditions and so on. Unless they adapt to these changes, they will not remain competitive and economically viable. They will fail ultimately.

In order to avoid failure, a business must have the means with which to adapt. It must have the ability to command resources, in the sense of disposing of existing resources and acquiring alternatives as and when this is necessary to its survival. Thus, at any particular point of time, a business holds a collection of resources in various forms in order to undertake particular tasks that have been determined by management as then relevant to its survival. If economic, technological or other conditions change and require a consequential alteration to its resource structure, it will have to have the means of making this alteration effectively.

The means of doing this is usually cash – unwanted resources being translated by sale (where possible) into cash, and the latter (plus any further cash available from operations, borrowing, etc.) being used to acquire the needed alternative resources. Cash is therefore an expression of command over resources, and the CFR system is a means of reporting on that command (and therefore on the adaptability of the entity).[41] It is based on a description of resources in cash terms using sale prices, and states specifically the cash flows that have been or are available to be generated from the realization of resources (in the Statements of Realized Cash Flow, Realizable Earnings, Financial Position, and Changes in Financial Position). With the added benefit of resources, liabilities and related flows being disclosed in order of realizability and payability, the report user is given clear information on the entity's command over resources in terms of cash, and thus of its adaptability in a changing environment.

It should be noted that this does not mean that specific adaptations are intended or expected. The use of sale prices in CFR is made in order to portray the general condition of adaptability rather than to comment on particular adaptations. The more adaptable the reporting entity is, the less likely it is to have its survival threatened in a rapidly changing world. Thus it is argued that report users are entitled to receive financial information that reflects on this risk in terms of the realizability of the entity's assets (using sale prices). The latter should not be read as intentions to liquidate assets; merely to report how easily and to what extent the latter could be converted into the cash resources needed to adapt from one business form into another.

These are therefore crucial matters for report users concerned with the ultimate survival of the entity. Some businesses are bound to be less adaptable than others because of their lack of command over resources due to both the realizability and the sale prices associated with their existing resource structure. For example, it appears reasonable to suggest that retail concerns may be somewhat more adaptable than manufacturing concerns. CFR would highlight these differences in terms of realized and realizable cash flows and net assets. For example:

Assume YZ owns a stage-coach business at a time when stage coaches were the main means of public transportation. Assume also a CFR system of reporting with the following statements in cash or cash equivalent terms:

STATEMENT OF REALIZED CASH FLOW
Year to 31 December

	1878	*1879*	*1880*	*1881*	*1882*	*Total*
	£000	*£000*	*£000*	*£000*	*£000*	*£000*
Cash inflows						
Operating cash flow	5	12	4	4	2	27
Decrease in cash asset	1	–	4	–	2	7
	6	12	8	4	4	34
Cash outflows						
Capital expenditure	–	5	3	–	–	8
Distribution paid	6	5	5	4	4	24
Increase in cash asset	–	2	–	–	–	2
	6	12	8	4	4	34

STATEMENT OF REALIZABLE EARNINGS
Year to 31 December

	1878 *£000*	*1879* *£000*	*1880* *£000*	*1881* *£000*	*1882* *£000*	*Total* *£000*
Realized earnings						
Operating cash flow	5	12	4	4	2	27
Unrealized earnings						
Readily-realizable net assets:						
Horses	(3)	(4)	(2)	(4)	(1)	(14)
Stocks of feedstuffs	1	1	—	1	—	3
Stage coaches	(12)	(16)	—	—	—	(28)
(Creditors)	—	1	1	(1)	1	2
	(14)	(18)	(1)	(4)	—	(37)
Not-readily-realizable assets:						
Stage coaches	—	—	(6)	(4)	(3)	(13)
Stables and offices	(5)	(5)	—	—	—	(10)
	(5)	(5)	(6)	(4)	(3)	(23)
	(14)	(11)	(3)	(4)	(1)	(33)
Less: distribution provided	5	5	4	4	4	22
	(19)	(16)	(7)	(8)	(5)	(55)
Add: retained earnings of prior periods	70	51	35	28	20	70
Retained earnings carried forward	51	35	28	20	15	15

STATEMENT OF FINANCIAL POSITION
Year to 31 December

	1877 *£000*	*1878* *£000*	*1879* *£000*	*1880* *£000*	*1881* *£000*	*1882* *£000*
Cash asset						
Bank	7	6	8	4	4	2
Readily-realizable assets						
Horses	21	18	19	20	16	15
Stock of feedstuffs, etc.	3	4	5	5	6	6
Stage coaches	42	30	14	—	—	—
	66	52	38	25	22	21
Less: short-term liabilities						
Creditors	7	7	6	5	6	5
Distribution	6	5	5	4	4	4
	13	12	11	9	10	9
	53	40	27	16	12	12

Not-readily-realizable assets						
Stage coaches	—	—	—	8	4	1
Stables and offices	20	15	10	10	10	10
	20	15	10	18	14	11
	80	61	45	38	30	25
Owner's equity						
Capital	10	10	10	10	10	10
Retained earnings	70	51	35	28	20	15
	80	61	45	38	30	25

The above CFR statements have been based on the data contained in Appendix 5 (the Statement of Changes in Financial Position is not produced as it is not absolutely essential to the discussion). The statements reflect the decline of the stage coach business in terms that matter most to its survival – that is, cash flow.

The business is dying rapidly owing to technological change. It is imperative that it adapt to meet this challenge in order to survive. The CFR figures reveal the need to adapt and reflect the lack of adaptation. Operating cash flows have been small and declining (£27,000 in total). They have been supplemented by a net reduction in the bank balance of £5,000, and used almost exclusively for distributions (£24,000 in total). In other words, the business has not been adapting by utilizing available cash to acquire alternative resources – in fact, a small amount of £8,000 was spent on necessary replacements of existing resources.

The Statement of Realizable Earnings reflects the profitability of the business more fully – although £27,000 has been realized in the form of operating cash flows, potential losses in non-monetary assets of £60,000 (£37,000 concerning readily-realizable assets, and £23,000 for not-readily-realizable assets) have resulted in aggregate sale price-based losses before distribution in each of the five years (£33,000 in total). Thus, the business has witnessed a considerable reduction in the sale prices of its realizable assets, at the same time as it has failed to utilize available cash to acquire an alternative asset structure.

This deteriorating situation is confirmed in the Statement of Financial Position. Certain resources (horses and stocks of feedstuffs) have remained relatively marketable throughout the five-year period; thus providing some means of adaptability to the business. However, other major assets (stage coaches and property) have become increasingly unrealizable, as well as less valuable in cash terms, and thereby reduced the entity's adaptability and command over resources. At the end of 1877, it had £80,000 of cash or cash-equivalent net assets (75% of which were in realized or readily-realizable form). By the end of 1882, the corresponding figures were £25,000 and 56%, respectively.

The CFR system therefore has the considerable potential to inform a business' owners of the adaptability of the reporting entity and its command over alternative resources. It can also provide related information to other interested report user groups, but particularly to lenders, bankers and suppliers concerned with the entity's ability to meet repayments when due, and the assets available to secure the relevant debts. In the case of YZ, each of these groups should be concerned at the decreasing adaptability of the business. But each should also be anxious about declining viability and asset structure. The two groups concerned in this case would be the bank and creditors.

Both of these interested groups could note from the sale price-based financial statements several relevant cash flow features – first, the diminishing operating cash flow, in most years producing only a small surplus; second, the use of the available cash flow in each year to meet distributions rather than needed capital expenditure; third, the rapid decline in cash equivalents for readily-realizable assets, thus providing less and less cash cover for the debt due; and, fourth, the gradual erosion of available cash assets. Thus, although the business has managed to meet its debt repayments when due and to provide cash-equivalent cover for its debts, the situation by 31 December 1882 is one that could rapidly deteriorate into operational cash flow deficits and eventual insolvency. These matters are seen clearly in CFR terms, and the relevant financial statements are designed specifically to meet the needs of groups such as YZ's bankers and creditors.

MANAGERIAL ACCOUNTABILITY

One of the original purposes of external financial reporting was to provide a means by which management could be made to account to ownership for its stewardship of the resources entrusted to it by the latter. Such an accounting objective exists today, although its importance appears to have been diminished considerably by the attention paid to the decision needs of report users. Arguably, however, managerial accountability ought to remain as a significant aim of financial reporting – formal accounting statements appear to be a useful way of ensuring that management conveys relevant messages about the way in which it has exercised custody over the resources given to it; and, specifically, the uses to which these resources have been put and the financial consequences of these uses.

CFR appears to be a system of accounting and reporting that is suited ideally to the accountability objective. In clear, unambiguous and objective terms, it provides information not only on the resources of the business being managed, but also on the consequences of such resource management. Specifically, it is concerned to report on the financial management of the entity – that is, the ways and means by which the available resources have been utilized profitability to provide returns for those persons who have invested in the entity. The terms in which such an accounting is described are those of cash, cash equivalent and cash flow, and cash is the factor central to financial management – profits require to be translated into cash flows to provide the cash needed to acquire resources, repay obligations, and provide returns.

CFR is also a system of accounting and reporting that has a universal appeal in the sense of providing information needed by various groups (including owners, lenders, bankers, suppliers, employees, customers and government). Thus, the cash flow-based reports appear to satisfy the function of accountability in its wider modern form which includes most groups of persons who can be classed as stake-holders in the entity. All such groups ought to be concerned about the quality of management generally, and financial management particularly. Each can be injured by failures either at the general or specific levels. CFR therefore contains information relevant to assessing the quality of management by any of these groups. This can be illustrated with reference to the data used in the case of YZ in the previous section (see also Appendix 5).

At 31 December 1877, the management of the business was responsible for a net asset structure comprising realized, readily-realizable and not-readily-realizable resources with a total cash equivalent of £80,000. By 31 December 1882, the structure had diminished to a cash equivalent figure of £25,000 in a much less readily-realizable form. This can be evidenced in the relevant Statement of Financial Position. The reason for this change is to be seen in, first, the Statement of Realized Cash Flow and, second, the Statement of Realizable Earnings – a relatively small amount of additional cash inflow has been realized from operating (£27,000) and has been used mainly to finance distributions (£24,000), whereas non-cash net assets have decreased in cash equivalent terms by £60,000. These figures appear to indicate a management of poor quality that has not adapted to the operational changes required in the business and that, instead, has preferred to run down the entity by lack of relevant capital expenditure and by over-distribution.

OTHER POINTS

The system of CFR specified in this text has certain qualities that are compatible with those typically sought by accounting policy-makers.

Relevance[42]

CFR-based information is relevant to the needs of various report-user groups. This point has been made several times previously, and will not be repeated at length at this stage. Suffice to say that cash flow and cash equivalent data appear to be matters that relate closely to most information needs. In this respect, CFR has a universality not easily evidenced in other forms of accounting information.[43]

Correspondence

CFR information attempts to correspond to economic reality as factually as possible – that is, if it is felt to be desirable that reported information represents that reality without unnecessary distortion, then CFR appears suitable. Its use of cash flows and sale prices, free from the subjective judgments of periodic cost allocations and the uncertainties of accruals, makes it a system which is reasonably objective. It also utilizes a measurement scale, based on sale prices, that is additive and provides aggregates and matchings that are meaningful – that is, in the sense that all measured data are expressed in cash or cash-equivalent terms. Thus cash flows can be added to, subtracted from or matched with cash flows if all are expressed in the purchasing power terms of the same reporting period. Similarly, sale prices expressed at the same point of time can be added to, subtracted from or matched with other sale prices of the same point of time. The avoidance of time allocations minimizes the uncertainties resulting from an accounting for arbitrarily measured data. Although not eliminating subjectivity entirely from the financial reporting function, CFR does appear to introduce a greater degree of objectivity in the measurement process than is the case with allocation-based systems.

Comparability

Because of its use of reasonably objective data, and its avoidance of subjective judgments, CFR provides information that ought to be comparable, at least at the same point of time. The objective nature of the measurements necessary to produce CFR data make comparisons valid so long as the time period is held constant. It also can be concluded reasonably that CFR introduces a consistency in accounting method that aids greatly the quality of informational comparability.

Comprehension

It can be argued that CFR information, because of its dependence on cash flows and sale prices, is a system of accounting and reporting that ought to be understood by the non-accountant user of financial reports. There is evidence to support the view that the latter may well think in terms of cash flows and sale prices when presented with statements of profitability and financial position.[44] It is therefore to his advantage to receive information that matches his perception and intuition.

Going concern

One of the most generally accepted and consistently applied conventions in traditional accounting is that of going concern – that is, the assumption when applying accounting practices to recorded data that the reporting entity has an indefinite life, and that there is therefore no forseeable ending of that life. This convention has dominated accounting thought in relation to such matters as stock valuation and fixed asset depreciation. Despite its use of sale prices, CFR does not breach this convention – the use of sale prices does not signal a realization of the assets nor a liquidation of the entity. Instead, it conveys the message that assets could be transformed, as and when required, into alternative forms by means of sale and subsequent acquisition. The entity, under these circumstances of gradual adaptation to change, is the permanent feature (the going concern). Its asset structure is the factor liable to change when necessary. Sale prices reflect the adaptability of the asset structure, and the risks associated with the entity remaining a going concern. Thus, CFR relates to the entity concept as much as any other financial reporting system. By concentrating on the continuity of the entity rather than its operations or resource structure, much of the confusions over the interpretation of the entity concept in traditional practice are avoided.[45]

CHAPTER 7 Analysis of actual cash flows

The claims made for CFR in this text, and particularly those outlined in Chapter 6, remain as no more than arguments until CFR can be demonstrated to be of practical benefit to financial report users. To provide such a demonstration is the purpose of this and the following chapters. In particular, a system of CFA analysis is explained that provides a means of obtaining evidence of entity financial performance for the report user. The system proposed is based on ideas for analysis introduced in Chapter 6, but is not described in specific user terms as individual users would wish to select those elements of greatest relevance to their particular needs.

The system of analysis is limited largely to CFR data because the latter are the subject of the text. However, this should not be taken to imply that other forms of financial analysis are to be disregarded. Financial analysis depends on as many sources of relevant information as possible, although the comments made earlier concerning cost allocation-based data should not be ignored.

This chapter describes the analysis of realized cash flows, and relates this, in part, to the conventional analysis of historic cost-based information in order to demonstrate the additional contribution made by CFR-based data to entity assessments. Chapter 8 extends the analysis to sale price-based information, and thus examines the use of realized and unrealized cash flows to assess entity performance. As in each of the previous chapters, the text is supported by worked examples. The data upon which the latter have been based are described in the first instance in historic cost terms in Appendix 6.

PROFITABILITY AND LIQUIDITY

The most significant feature of realized cash flow analysis is its specific attention to the liquidity position of the reporting entity, and the conversion of realized profits into cash flows available to fund expenditure. This is a matter that has been commented on at several points in the text, and it will be used as the basis for the remainder of the discussion and explanation in this chapter. In particular, the analysis of realized cash flows is an attempt to provide in summary and aggregate terms certain of the liquidity features of the reporting entity that are examined conventionally in a series of specific and separate financial ratios. It provides an essential overview of the periodic changes in liquidity position that have resulted from the financial management of the entity.

If the report user is to provide meaningful interpretations of entity financial performance from which rational decisions can be made, it is necessary for him to judge such performance not just in the generally accepted terms of profitability, but also on the basis of liquidity. As argued earlier, profits are a vital element of entity survival, but, unless there is also a related cash inflow from trading operations to finance such matters as capital expenditure, taxation, dividends and borrowing repayments, then external funding will be required. A continuous lack of cash contributions from profitable operations will sooner or later bring about the demise of the entity. Thus, to judge the latter solely in terms of its profit performance is to take a very narrow view of its financial affairs, and ignore the elementary financial lesson demonstrated on several occasions in this text that profit and cash flow are not synonymous. To reinforce this point, the historic cost-based profit data for 1985 given in Appendix 6 are assumed as follows:

	£000
Sales	410
Less: cost of sales	329
	81
Less: other expenses	36
	45
Less: depreciation	13
	32
Less: taxation provided	13
	19
Less: dividend provided	8
Retained profit	11

The underlying and equivalent cash flow, however, is described by an alternative set of figures (the differences are due to such matters as stock, debtors and creditors, and will be explained later in this chapter):

	£000
Sales received	387
Less: payments for goods for sale	333
	54
Less: other expenses paid	32
	22
Less: capital expenditure	20
	2
Less: taxation paid	14
	(12)
Less: dividend paid	7
Increase in borrowing	(19)

In other words, the reported profit before depreciation of £45,000 had a cash flow equivalent of £22,000 and, whereas £11,000 of realized profit was retained to fund its activities, the entity increased its borrowing by £19,000.

An analysis of realized cash flows concentrates on the second rather than the first set of figures, and attempts to provide the report user with a means of evidencing actual and potential cash flow achievement. However, before this can be done, it is important to provide a framework for analysis that will describe fairly the cash flow performance of the reporting entity. The need for this to be done can be evidenced by examining further the cash flow figures given above.

The figures are given in the form of a statement of cash-based surplus, and thereby suggest or imply a measure of financial performance in terms of profitability. The statement is similar in design to the conventional profit statement. In addition, it infers the possibility of distributions (£7,000) being funded by borrowings because of the ordering and matching of the individual terms in the report – in other words, a substitution of debt for equity. For example, the matching suggests that, after deduction of capital expenditure of £20,000 only £2,000 of operating cash flow remained to cover taxation and dividend payments of £14,000 and £7,000, respectively. In particular, this infers that the additional borrowing of £19,000 was used to fund £12,000 of tax and £7,000 of dividends. This may have been the case, but it is impossible for the report user to reach this conclusion without further information being available as to the purpose and actual use of borrowing (and this is unlikely to be the case).

An alternative and less ambiguous cash flow structure would appear to be required – that is, one that is useful to a wide range of report users interested in the vital issue of entity liquidity; emphasizes liquidity performance rather than profitability; and avoids dubious matchings of cash inflows and outflows. Such a format has been used in Chapter 5 and elsewhere in this text when the reporting structure of a CFR system has been considered. It is now discussed within the context of analysing CFR data.

Using the figures used above, the following statement attempts to comply with these criteria:

	£
Operating cash flow	22,000
Aditional borrowing	19,000
	41,000
Capital expenditure	20,000
Taxation payments	14,000
Dividend payments	7,000
	41,000

The emphasis is on a 'pool' of cash (in this sense, £41,000) – partly generated internally (operating cash flow of £22,000) and partly generated from external sources (borrowings of £19,000). The 'pool' has been used for internal reinvestment (£20,000 on capital expenditure) and external distribution (taxation of £14,000 and dividends of £7,000). It avoids, particularly, potentially misleading inferences about the financing of specific outflows. Instead, it attempts to describe unambiguously all major inflows and outflows of the reporting entity – with the emphasis on avoiding arguable matchings of data for analysis purposes.

INTERPRETATION

It is important to explain at this stage how the above cash flow reporting format may be interpreted generally by the report user. Much of this is obviously a matter of personal judgement for any user, but there do appear to be several unique features of the system that ought to be introduced.

The first point to be considered is that of cash inflow. In a typical and usual situation not involving new equity capital or reductions in existing cash assets, this will reveal how much cash in the stated reporting period has been generated from operations and how much has come from net additional borrowings. In the example being used, the figures were £22,000 and £19,000, respectively. The figures for borrowings could, if desired, be split between short-term and longer-term amounts. However, of particular concern in the typical situation of cash inflow is the relationship between operating cash flow and additional borrowing. This describes how much of the total inflow has been generated internally from the trading operations of the reporting entity, and how much has come from external sources such as bankers and lenders.

The relating of cash inflows in this way is an unconventional approach to examining changes in the financial structure of the reporting entity. In incremental terms, its cash funding from operations is compared with that from external sources. For this purpose, it is important for cash flows to be compared with cash flows for analysis purposes – that is, the data are expressed in the same measurement terms. This is not the case in the nearest equivalent conventional analysis of gearing when comparisons are made in absolute terms of aggregate borrowing with cumulative capital and retained profits – borrowings representing cash or cash-equivalent inflows, but equity being subject to accounting accrual and allocation procedures. Similarly, it can be argued that the cash-based financing comparison is more dynamic and objective than its conventional counterpart because of its use of incremental data and its avoidance of accounting judgements in its measurement. For example, in the previous example, the operating cash flow figure of £22,000 was equivalent to a profit before depreciation of £45,000 after exclusion of an increase in working capital (defined as stock plus debtors minus creditors) of £23,000. Thus, the cash flow figure of £22,000 was free of the subjectivity of the accruals and allocations of depreciation, stock, debtors and creditors, and was a net measurement of cash received from customers of £387,000 minus cash paid to suppliers, employees and other providers of services of £365,000.

Comparing the incremental cash flow figures for operations and borrowing, the report user is able to examine relevant figures that describe how much the entity has been contributing in cash terms to its survival. For example, too little cash flow from operations and too much from additional borrowing, particularly over several years, are indicators of actual and/or potential liquidity problems. It is a situation that reveals a possible lack of operational viability and provides evidence for the analyst of the entity's lack of potential to generate sufficient cash to meet its expenditure requirements. For example, a lack of operating cash flow today, compensated for by borrowing, means future operating cash flows being diminished by the cost of servicing debt, which, in turn, may increase borrowing, and so on in a downward cash flow spiral.

So far as cash outflows are concerned, the analysis is similar to the above in principle. It attempts to describe how much of the total cash available has been used to invest in capital expenditure of use in the trading operations of the entity; pay for taxation when due; make distributions to owners; and, on occasion, increase cash assets or reduce existing borrowings. In addition, if the cost of interest on borrowings is substantial, the report user may wish to treat interest as a separate outflow with operating cash flow described before deduction of such expenditure. (For purposes of simplification of the analysis in this chapter, interest costs have not been separated.)

With the analysis of cash outflows in the usual case involving mainly those concerned with investment and distribution (in its widest sense), the analyst would be examining for levels of investment adequate to provide operating cash flows in the future; the size of the return to government in the form of taxation payments; and a justifiable level of distribution to owners of the entity. For example, too little investment, coupled with high levels of taxation and over-generous distributions, are ingredients for potential cash flow problems. The quantified situation used previously discloses £20,000 spent on investment, £14,000 on tax, and £7,000 on dividends. Thus, the majority of available cash in this period (£21,000) had flowed out of the entity with no prospect of any direct return from it in the future. Subject to the circumstances of the entity and the nature of its operations, repetition of these figures over several years could prove damaging to its prospects of generating adequate operating cash flows – the more cash is spent on relatively 'unproductive' payments such as tax and dividends, the more likely the entity is to have future operating cash flows that will require supplementing by borrowing or new capital.

The suggested 'fund'-based format for disclosure and analysis of realized cash flow is designed to facilitate for the report user an overview of significant changes in the reporting entity's liquidity position as a result of its financial management. Because it provides for an analysis in strictly cash terms, it avoids many of the problems associated with conventional analysis, particularly those concerning accounting flexibility caused by subjective judgements due to allocations and accruals. For example, assume the situation and figures used previously with the additional information that the closing stock valuation had been increased by £9,000 due to a fixed overhead allocation by management, and closing debtors had been reduced by £3,000 due to the creation of a general provision for bad debts. Profit before depreciaion would be increased £6,000 to £51,000[a] and the increase in working capital for the period also would be increased by the same amount to £29,000[b]. Subtracting the latter datum from the former provides proof that the operating cash flow of £22,000 has remained unaffected. In other words, no matter what judgements are made with regard to the measurement of profit, CFR data remain as they were constituted at the time of each cash transaction. The cash flow underlying profit is an objective measure even if it has been distorted by managerial manipulation of the timing of specific cash inflows and outflows.

DEVELOPING CFR-BASED ANALYSES

The next thing to be said about the analysis of realized cash flows is that entities do not report at the present time in cash flow terms. There is no specific accounting or legal requirement to produce a realized cash flow statement of the type described in previous chapters. However, this should not prevent the report user producing required cash flow data when they are not immediately available. He can do so by making use of the present source and application of funds statement. In this report, the report user will find typically that funds data are largely in cash terms and that, with a minimum of further adjustments, all data can be described in cash terms and thereby be available for placing within the analysis format described above.

The adjustments required to put a funds statement in a cash format are largely a matter of rearrangement and arithmetic. The exact format of the funds statement can vary according to the specific circumstances of the reporting entity – for example, borrowing receipts may be disclosed as a source of funds with repayments shown as an application of funds – alternatively, the net change in borrowing may be presented as one figure; working capital (defined for this purpose as stock plus debtors minus creditors) may have increased and this will be shown as an application of funds – on the other hand, a decrease may appear as either a source or negative application. The basic cash flow principle, however, is to rearrange whatever have been disclosed as funds data in order to derive the cash flow equivalent figures.

In order to translate a funds statement to a cash basis usually requires a suitable matching of reported profits adjusted for non-cash items such as depreciation and the periodic working capital change in order to derive operating cash flow: that is, deduct from profit an increase in working capital or add a decrease. Applying the figures used previously, profit before depreciation was £45,000 and the increase in working capital was £23,000, giving an operating cash flow of £22,000. If the change in working capital had been a reduction, the operating cash flow would have been £68,000[c].

The effect of this adjustment, which is founded on a reversal of the conventional effects of double-entry bookkeeping, is to remove from the cash flow model any increase or decrease in realized profit caused by an equivalent movement in working capital. Thus, as mentioned previously, it removes much of the subjectivity inherent in accounting profit measurements.

However, it also has the potential disadvantage of assuming all debtors and creditors relate to revenue items rather than, say, capital expenditure. Much depends on the level of disclosure in financial statements available to the report user but, nevertheless, such adjustments appear to provide reasonable approximations of actual cash flows from operations.

Other funds statement adjustments may be necessary if cash flow data are not available and require to be derived. For example, in order to simplify the cash flow format, it is possible to net capital expenditure with relatively insignificant disposal proceeds of fixed assets and related government grants. This gives a figure for net cash investment. In similar vein, the report user may find it easier to identify borrowing cash flows by aggregating the various short and longer-term borrowings and netting off against any repayments. On the other hand, it must be remembered that such nettings can hide material inflows and outflows. This is an area the analyst must approach with care and caution.

The various funds statement adjustments can be seen in the following illustration, using the following fund statement derived from the data contained in Appendix 6.

	1980	*1981*	*1982*	*1983*	*1984*	*1985*
	£000	*£000*	*£000*	*£000*	*£000*	*£000*
Source of funds						
Profit before tax	8	16	23	24	25	32
Add: depreciation	5	5	8	11	13	13
	13	21	31	35	38	45
Increase in creditors	1	10	3	3	17	14
	14	31	34	38	55	59
Application of funds						
Fittings purchased	—	—	15	15	10	20
Dividends paid	2	2	4	6	7	7
Taxation paid	2	4	8	10	10	14
Increase in stock	2	10	5	3	18	14
Increase in debtors	8	17	16	18	21	23
	14	33	48	52	66	78
Increase in overdraft	—	2	14	14	11	19

The first step is to calculate the operating cash flow for each year:

	1980 *£000*	*1981* *£000*	*1982* *£000*	*1983* *£000*	*1984* *£000*	*1985* *£000*
Profit before depreciation	13	21	31	35	38	45
Less: increase in working capital:						
stock	2	10	5	3	18	14
debtors	8	17	16	18	21	23
(creditors)	(1)	(10)	(3)	(3)	(17)	(14)
	9	17	18	18	22	23
Operating cash flow	4	4	13	17	16	22

As there are no further nettings to be undertaken (for example, with capital expenditure and borrowing), the remaining data can be ranged in the cash flow format recommended:

	1980 *£000*	*1981* *£000*	*1982* *£000*	*1983* *£000*	*1984* *£000*	*1985* *£000*
Operating cash flow	4	4	13	17	16	22
Borrowing	–	2	14	14	11	19
	4	6	27	31	27	41
Capital expenditure	–	–	15	15	10	20
Taxation paid	2	4	8	10	10	14
Dividends paid	2	2	4	6	7	7
	4	6	27	31	27	41

Thus, the realized cash flow data for analysis are now available. The relative complexity and lack of structure of the funds statement has been reduced to a relative few figures describing inflows and outflows. Cash inflows reflect the realized cash flow from operations after working capital requirements have been met, and as augmented by additional borrowing. Cash outflows portray cash spent on capital expenditure, and therefore put back into the business, and cash paid to external sources in the form of taxation and dividends.

As such, the above statement of realized cash flow (whether disclosed directly or derived from a funds statement) provides the report user with financial data in cash terms that reflect the influence of the actions of its financial management (in terms of the effect of working capital investment or disinvestment on cash flow available from realized profit; the relative dependence or independence of the entity on external funding from borrowing; and the use of available cash to reinvest, pay for tax due, and make distributions to owners). For these reasons, and as argued previously, the realized cash flow data capture much of the essential and basic changes in the liquidity position of the reporting entity.

FURTHER PREPARATION

An obvious feature of realized cash flow data is that they lack the 'smoothness' of accrual and allocation-based accounting measurements such as realized profit figures. This is due to the inevitable lumpiness of timing involved in particular receipts and payments. Specific periods of entity activity can be subject to significant increases or decreases in operating cash flow owing to working capital changes involving stock, debtors and creditors; investment in capital expenditure can be of an ad hoc nature depending on when fixed assets need replaced; borrowing receipts and repayments occur when funding is required or can be reduced; and taxation payments depend in part on the incidence of particular transactions in past periods. The fluctuations inherent in cash flows presumably are a major reason for the extensive use of accrual and allocation techniques in conventional accounting, and cause problems for the report user if his examination of realized cash flows is limited to a series of individual years particularly if an individual year is influenced significantly by the incidence of particular cash transactions.

It is therefore suggested that the report user can avoid using only twelve-monthly reported realized cash flows and, instead, construct multi-period aggregates to provide a series of cash flow results that is not affected unduly by those of a single period. In doing so, it is argued that the user should be reflecting in his multi-period analysis the natural trading cycle of the reporting entity.[46] For example, the following are the figures for operating cash flow described above:

1980	*1981*	*1982*	*1983*	*1984*	*1985*
£000	*£000*	*£000*	*£000*	*£000*	*£000*
4	4	13	17	16	22

Although these figures are increasing over time, there are fluctuations (jumping from £4,000 in 1981 to £13,000 in 1982, and reducing from £17,000 in 1983 to £16,000 in 1984). Assuming for illustrative purposes a three-year trading cycle, a multi-period presentation can be given:

	1980–2	*1981–3*	*1982–4*	*1983–5*
	£000	*£000*	*£000*	*£000*
Operating cash flow (d)	21	34	46	55

From the above series, the report user is able to confirm its upwards direction from £21,000 in the first three-year period to £55,000 in the last. However, he is able to detect relatively easily the slowing down of the increase – £13,000 between the first two periods, to £12,000 between the next two, and further down to £9,000 between the last two. The figures are not too difficult to interpret in this case, but it could be the case that fluctuations of specific cash flows mask the underlying trend.

Much will depend on the reporting entity's operating cycle as to what multi-period is chosen for analysis purposes. That of a retail concern may be only one or two years, whereas that of a manufacturer may extend to four or five years. Knowledge of the nature of the entity's operations is therefore essential. But a skilled report user would be expected to have it.[47] In any case, the multi-period aggregates should be seen as complementary to the single-period figures.

The final aspect of the preparation of realized cash flow data for analysis purposes concerns the presentation of them in a way that aids the report user to examine changes in the overall liquidity position of the reporting entity as easily as possible. To this end, it is recommended that the aggregate figures could be put in the form of percentage contributions. In order to do this, the multi-period data should be prepared:

	1980–2	*1981–3*	*1982–4*	*1983–5*	*1980–5*
	£000	*£000*	*£000*	*£000*	*£000*
Operating cash flow (e)	21	34	46	55	76
Borrowing (f)	16	30	39	44	60
	37	64	85	99	136
Capital expenditure (g)	15	30	40	45	60
Taxation paid (h)	14	22	28	34	48
Dividends (i)	8	12	17	20	28
	37	64	85	99	136

Once this is done, the data can be put in percentage form (each percentage being based on the total flow for the period concerned):

	1980–2	*1981–3*	*1982–4*	*1983–5*	*1980–5*
	%	%	%	%	%
Operating cash flow (j)	57	53	54	56	56
Borrowing (k)	43	47	46	44	44
	100	100	100	100	100
Capital expenditure (l)	40	47	47	46	44
Taxation paid (m)	38	34	33	34	35
Dividends paid (n)	22	19	20	20	21
	100	100	100	100	100

Thus, from this overall statement, the report user has an overview of developments in the liquidity position of the reporting entity. Despite the annual increases and decreases in certain individual inflows and outflows that were evident (for example, those affecting operating cash flow, borrowing and capital expenditure); and the apparent constancy of periodic increases in others (such as taxation and dividends), the series of figures is much more stable when examined over the six-year period. The entity has been contributing consistently approximately 56% of needed cash from its operations with the remainder coming from additional borrowings. Borrowings have therefore remained at a continuously high level. A sizeable minority of available cash has been used for capital expenditure, with a slightly smaller proportion forming taxation payments. One fifth of available cash has been distributed consistently in the form of dividends. Many different interpretations can be made of these figures. But several points of general importance can be attributed to them.

In order to aid these explanations, the data that have been used throughout this chapter are related to their historic cost equivalents given in outline in Appendix 6.

LONGER-TERM DEVELOPMENTS

The first point to make is that the emphasis in the analysis of realized cash flows is on long-term development of cash flow and liquidity matters – in this case, examining six years of data in three-year 'rolling' totals. It therefore goes much beyond the traditional assessments of liquidity that tend to be static in terms of examining positions at discrete points of time. Realized cash flow analysis views liquidity as a condition of the entity to be examined over time. In particular, it corresponds to the reality of cash flow problems. They do not develop at points of time; instead, they occur over time, and it is this development with which the report user should be concerned – to spot early signs of long-term cash flow problems such as the generation of insufficient cash flow from operations, or an over-generous distribution of cash flow to entity owners.

For example, using the data given in Appendix 6, the following conventional liquidity-related ratios can be produced:

	1980	*1981*	*1982*	*1983*	*1984*	*1985*
Working capital ratio* (o)	1.5	1.5	1.3	1.3	1.3	1.2
Quick ratio* (p)	1.0	1.0	0.9	0.9	0.8	0.8

* including the bank overdraft, and taxation and dividend provisions.

These ratios reveal an apparently declining overall liquidity position for the reporting entity. Thus, the 20% decline in both ratios between 1980 and 1985 may be a point of concern for the report user. However, the analysis of realized cash flows provides objective evidence that, despite such a decline, the rate of increase in realized profit between 1980 and 1985 has been such as to ensure a reasonable constancy in the balance between operating cash flow and additional borrowing contributions.

A more detailed conventional analysis of working capital items reveals a further narrow interpretation of financial events. For example, the following 'turnover' ratios can be derived from the figures given in Appendix 6:

(all figures months)	*1980*	*1981*	*1982*	*1983*	*1984*	*1985*
Stock turnover (q)	2.0	1.9	1.8	1.8	1.8	1.9
Debtors turnover (r)	2.3	2.6	2.6	3.2	3.2	3.0
Creditors turnover (s)	1.7	1.6	1.6	1.6	1.6	1.7

Irrespective of the deterioration in debtors turnover (by approximately one half month of credit between 1980 and 1985), this has not changed substantially the operating cash flow contribution of the entity over the six-year period (or at least its effect has been relatively small). The major point of the analysis of realized cash flows in this case is to reveal the lack of significant influence on cash flow of the slow-down of debtors turnover. In other words, conventional ratio analysis goes some way to identifying long-term cash flow problems relating to entity operations. Cash flow-based analysis attempts to combine the influence of the separately identified parts of conventional analysis. It provides an overview of the net result of the financial management of profits, stocks, debtors and creditors.

The same can be said of entity distributions. The relevant figures in Appendix 6 provide the following dividend covers:

	1980	*1981*	*1982*	*1983*	*1984*	*1985*
Dividend cover (t)	2.0	2.0	2.2	2.0	1.6	2.4

These fluctuating ratios relate specifically to profitability and distribution. As dividends are presumably determined as much by the availability of cash flow as profit, the analysis of realized cash flows reveals the cash outflow of dividends in absolute and proportional terms – in the example, an average amounting to approximately one fifth of available cash. Thus, although dividend provisions have quadrupled to £8,000 between 1980 and 1985, the realized cash flow data do not suggest that dividend payments have been an increasing proportion of available cash flow.

Finally, a traditional analysis of profitability as expressed in the figures presented in Appendix 6 might involve the following ratios:

	1980	*1981*	*1982*	*1983*	*1984*	*1985*
	%	*%*	*%*	*%*	*%*	*%*
Gross profit margin (u)	23.8	23.8	23.8	23.6	21.1	19.8
Net profit margin* (v)	9.5	12.3	11.2	10.1	8.4	7.8
Return on average capital* (w)	13.1	21.8	26.0	25.1	22.5	24.9

* expressed before taxation

Both the gross and net profit margins have therefore been declining over the six-year period (by approximately 18% between 1980 and 1985). On the other hand, the return on average capital has almost doubled between 1980 (at 13.1%) and 1985 (at 24.9%). But these figures only express part of the profitability picture. They do not and are not intended to describe the cash flow contributions from realized profits during the period. In fact, £183,000[x] of realized profits before depreciation contributed £76,000[y] of operating cash flow (operating working capital of stock, debtors minus creditors increasing by £107,000)[z].

LINKING OF RELATED MATTERS

As previously mentioned, an analysis of liquidity matters on a cash flow basis draws together various aspects of entity financial performance. It is concerned specifically with changes in the liquidity position of the entity because these are absolutely crucial to its survival in the short and long-term. It has the advantage of reflecting the influences of various factors on that liquidity position – for example, the realized profits of the entity; the financial management of working capital investment; the need to fund entity operations at least partly by borrowing; the impact of government-determined taxation policies and the ability of management to minimize its financial effects; and the distribution policy of management. All these matters should be subject to the attention of the report user, and the proposed analysis provides a means of examining their overall and combined cash flow effect over time.

Many of the previous examples in this chapter have illustrated these points but the following may summarize them:

(1) As mentioned in the previous section, realized profits for the six years of £183,000 generated £76,000 of operating cash flow after additional operating working capital investment of £107,000.
(2) Borrowing increased over the same six-year period by £60,000 and, together with operating cash flows, provided £136,000[aa] of cash available to meet capital, taxation and dividend payments.
(3) Fixed assets depreciation for the six years totalled £55,000[bb]. Capital expenditure, on the other hand, amounted to £60,000[cc]. Similarly, taxation and dividend provisions were, respectively, £59,000[dd] and £34,000[ee]. The equivalent cash payments were, respectively, £48,000[ff] and £28,000[gg].

The analysis of realized cash flows is therefore the means by which the report user can interpret the cash flow equivalents of conventional accounting figures and, because the data in the analysis of realized cash flows are expressed in cash flow terms, they do not contain many of the subjective judgments that accountants are required to incorporate in reported figures of profitability and financial position. The realized cash flow figures are considerably more objective data for the report user concerned to analyse the financial performance of the reporting entity.

CONCLUDING REMARKS

The major purpose of this chapter has been to outline for the report user (whether he be a professional or an amateur) a means whereby he can be assisted in examining the liquidity of a reporting entity and its cash flow performance. Even if cash flow data are not available they can be derived from the funds statement and do not therefore involve a search for a new source of information.

Realized cash flow-based analysis concentrates on changes in and contributions to liquidity through time rather than specific features of liquidity at particular points of time. In essence, the analysis provides a liquidity overview for the report user. It does so in terms that are relevant to the business feature being examined (that is, cash flow). It therefore avoids many of the subjective judgements of conventional accounting; and takes a longer-term view of entity developments than does traditional analysis. Realized cash flow-based analysis, however, must be regarded as complementary to rather than an alternative to conventional analysis.

CHAPTER 8

Analysis of realizable earnings and financial position

Techniques of conventional financial analysis can be applied to the CFR data contained in the Statements of Realizable Earnings and Financial Position. In order to reduce the relative complexity of the reported data to a few indicators of financial performance, the analyst can prepare relevant ratios on a cash flow and sale price basis. Thus, return on capital employed, gearing and working capital ratios can be prepared using CFR data. The purpose of this chapter is briefly to prepare and explain these ratios. Appendix 7 contains the detailed data on which the analyses are based.

FURTHER ADJUSTMENTS

In order to reduce the data to manageable proportions, the following summaries of Appendix 7 have been made:

STATEMENT OF REALIZABLE EARNINGS
Year to 31 December

	1980	*1981*	*1982*	*1983*	*1984*	*1985*
	£000	*£000*	*£000*	*£000*	*£000*	*£000*
Realized earnings	4	4	13	17	16	22
Unrealized earnings	7	23	16	15	23	14
Realized earnings	11	27	29	32	39	36

STATEMENT OF FINANCIAL POSITION
at 31 December

	1979	*1980*	*1981*	*1982*	*1983*	*1984*	*1985*
	£000	*£000*	*£000*	*£000*	*£000*	*£000*	*£000*
Total assets	81	89	122	156	189	239	287
Less: short-term liabilities	18	21	39	60	78	110	143
Capital employed	63	68	83	96	111	129	144

PROFITABILITY RETURNS

Using a CFR system, the measures and indicators of profitability are described in terms of returns based on realized and unrealized cash flows. The realized return is represented by the operating cash flow (the analysis of which was dealt with largely in Chapter 7); and the unrealized return comprises the aggregate of net asset changes in sale price terms (and will be examined in detail in this chapter). The aggregation of both returns provides the total return of realizable earnings. Each of these elements provides a numerator for the 'return on capital' indicator of financial performance (the denominator either being the 'equity' base of owner's capital employed or the 'entity' base of total assets). Each of these ratios will be examined in turn but, first, the relationship between realized and unrealized earnings will be analysed.

REALIZED AND UNREALIZED RETURNS

Realized cash flows are certain and objective. On the other hand, unrealized cash flows are uncertain and subjective. The financial analyst should be concerned to examine the 'mix' of these flows in terms of the composition of total CFR-based earnings. Changes in the mix may reflect changes in the structure of the entity, and the nature and quality of its financial management. For example, an increasing proportion of realized cash flow and a decreasing proportion of unrealized cash flow may signal a deteriorating non-cash asset base or a change in emphasis in terms of the entity's operations. A reversal of this situation may indicate the development of entity operational facilities with realized cash flows to come. Whatever the situation, the analyst requires suitable CFR data related to the earnings mix. For this to happen, the figures given in the Summarized Statement of Realizable Earnings can be converted into a percentage form:

REALIZED AND UNREALIZED RETURNS
Year to 31 December

	1980	*1981*	*1982*	*1983*	*1984*	*1985*
	%	%	%	%	%	%
Realized earnings (a)	36	15	45	53	41	61
Unrealized earnings (b)	64	85	55	47	59	39
	100	100	100	100	100	100

Thus it can be seen in this case that the operating cash flow contribution has been rising significantly from 36% to 61% whereas that of unrealized cash flows has been declining from 64% tc 39%. This situation is encouraging from the point of view of the availability of cash for such matters as investment, taxation and distribution (investigated in Chapter 7) and may reflect the gradual adaptation of the entity, from one form of operation into another. But the disbenefit may be the gradual deterioration in the non-cash asset base with a consequential deterioration in future operating cash flows (a matter to be looked at in later ratios). The analyst would require to use these CFR data with other sources of relevant information about the entity.

TOTAL ASSETS AND CAPITAL EMPLOYED

In a manner similar to the previous comparative analysis of CFR returns, it is possible to examine the relationships inherent in the owner's capital employed (as stated above in the Summarized Statement of Financial Position). This would provide the analyst with an overall review of the development of the financial structure of the reporting entity in sale price terms – that is, its total assets compared with the funds with which the latter have been financed. As a means of doing this, the data can be converted into percentage form in order to improve their comprehensibility, and the following statement can be produced:

FINANCIAL POSITION
as at 31 December

	1979	*1980*	*1981*	*1982*	*1983*	*1984*	*1985*
	%	%	%	%	%	%	%
Total assets (c)	100	100	100	100	100	100	100
Less: short-term liabilities (d)	22	24	32	38	41	46	50
Capital employed (e)	78	76	68	62	59	54	50

In terms of sale prices expressed in constant price terms, therefore, the above tabulation reflects the various financial contributions to this structure, and the changes in these contributions which have taken place over the period concerned. Given that longer-term liabilities would be included where relevant, the statement is one that describes the overall development in the financial gearing of the entity. In this case, the contribution from short-term financing sources (including the bank) has risen significantly over the six-year period (from 22% in 1979 to 50% in 1985). Total cash equivalent assets increased by 254% from £81,000 in 1979 to £287,000 in 1985. However, the corresponding increase for short-term liabilities was 694%[f]; but that for capital employed was only 129%[g]. In other words, although the entity's overall command over resources has increased considerably in monetary terms over the six years, the financing received from short-term sources has increased at a nearly three-times faster rate, thereby resulting in a relatively small increase in the owner's command over resources. The reasons for these changes can be seen more clearly in the gearing ratio explained in the next section.

ENTITY GEARING

The gearing ratio expresses the relationship between owner's equity and longer-term debt. It describes the relative dependancies of the entity on these sources of finance. In a CFR system it reveals also the relationship in comparable terms between the command over resources provided by the entity's longer-term lending sources, and that provided by its owners in the form of capital and profit retentions. In the example used in this chapter, the bank overdraft is treated as longer-term debt (despite its legal status as short-term financing) for purposes of calculating a gearing position for the entity. Its existence and escalation over the six-year period justify this treatment. The required figures are as follows:

	1979	*1980*	*1981*	*1982*	*1983*	*1984*	*1985*
	£000	*£000*	*£000*	*£000*	*£000*	*£000*	*£000*
Bank overdraft	5	5	7	21	35	46	65
Capital employed	63	68	83	96	111	129	144
Long-term financing	68	73	90	117	146	175	209

These data can be converted into gearing ratios in terms of debt to debt plus equity:

	1979	*1980*	*1981*	*1982*	*1983*	*1984*	*1985*
	%	*%*	*%*	*%*	*%*	*%*	*%*
Gearing ratio (h)	7	7	8	18	24	26	31

Thus, the gearing ratio helps to explain the reason for the overall changes in financial structure commented on earlier in this section. In 1979, the overdraft comprised 7% of the total long-term financing. By 1985, the equivalent statistic was a more than four-fold increase to 32%. The consequences of this situation, and the further utility of a CFR-based reporting system, can be evidenced by examining the relationship between total assets (the potential cash flow cover for entity liabilities) and longer-term debt (in this case, the bank overdraft):

	1979	*1980*	*1981*	*1982*	*1983*	*1984*	*1985*
	£000	*£000*	*£000*	*£000*	*£000*	*£000*	*£000*
Total assets	81	89	122	156	189	239	287
Bank overdraft	5	5	7	21	35	46	65
Cover (i)	16.2	17.8	17.4	7.4	5.4	5.2	4.4

The potential cash flow cover for the bank overdraft has reduced steadily, therefore, from approximately 16 to 18 times in the first three years to little more than 4 times in 1985. Overall, security for the bank (expressed in relevant cash terms) has diminished considerably owing to the increased gearing position of the entity.

RATES OF RETURN

The previous sections have outlined the realized and unrealized cash flow returns earned by the entity, and explained its changing financial structure. This section deals with the relationships of the returns to this structure in terms of rates of return on total assets (an entity approach) and owner's capital employed (an equity approach). The numerators and denominators of such rates are consistently expressed in CFR terms, and thereby allow legitimate comparisons to be made. The ratios described below are based on the CFR data given in previous sections. They are indicators of the realized and unrealized cash flows returning to the entity from its cash flow-equivalent investment in assets.

ENTITY RETURNS

The total cash flow investment made by the entity at any point of time is expressed in the sale price-based asset aggregate. The cash flow return earned by the entity during each period is described either in its realized form of operating cash flow or in its realized and unrealized combination of total realizable earnings. In order to ensure that the returns are those of the entity, and capable of being matched with total assets, they require to be described in terms of cash flows before deduction of interest on borrowings. Thus, assuming interest costs as follows: 1980 = £1,000; 1981 = £1,000; 1982 = £1,000; 1983 = £3,000; 1984 = £6,000 and 1985 = £7,000, the following entity cash flow returns pertain:

	1980	*1981*	*1982*	*1983*	*1984*	*1985*
	£000	*£000*	*£000*	*£000*	*£000*	*£000*
Operating cash flows as previously expressed	4	4	13	17	16	22
Add: interest costs	1	1	1	3	6	7
Realized entity return	5	5	14	20	22	29
Total realizable earnings as previously expressed	11	27	29	32	39	36
Add: interest costs	1	1	1	3	6	7
Realized entity return	12	28	30	35	45	43

The figures can now be related to the total assets figures. However, in order to reflect the cash flow-based capital of the period to which each return is related, it is suggested that it ought to be the average capital which is used. In this case, taking a simple rather than weighted arithmetic average, the entity capital figures would be:

	1980	*1981*	*1982*	*1983*	*1984*	*1985*
	£000	*£000*	*£000*	*£000*	*£000*	*£000*
Total average assets (j)	85	106	139	173	214	263

It is now possible to produce two measures of profit performance on a CFR basis – each using internally consistent and matching data. The first examines the realized cash rate of return, and the second describes the wider and more uncertain realizable rate of return. Both rates describe the profit performance of the entity without the influence of its financing structure.

	1980	*1981*	*1982*	*1983*	*1984*	*1985*
	%	*%*	*%*	*%*	*%*	*%*
Realized rate of return (k)	5.9	4.7	10.1	11.6	10.3	11.0

The above figures reveal that the realized cash return has almost doubled between 1980 and 1985, and has stabilized approximately in the last four years at a figure of 10%. This is the rate before interest, investment, taxation and distribution. It can be compared with similar returns from alternative investments.

The realized rate of return is effectively an 'acid' test of profit return because it excludes unrealized cash flows. The realizable rate of return compensates for this omission:

	1980	*1981*	*1982*	*1983*	*1984*	*1985*
	%	*%*	*%*	*%*	*%*	*%*
Realizable rate of return (l)	14.1	26.4	21.6	20.2	21.0	16.3

The realizable rate of return increased from 14.1% in 1980 to stabilize at approximately 20% in 1982 to 1984, inclusive, but fell back to little more than 16% in 1985. This return includes the less certain unrealized net sale price changes, and is expressed before interest, taxation and distribution. It would require to be assessed with comparable returns to judge its full meaning in the context of the situation being examined.

EQUITY RETURNS

In order to assess the rates of return earned by the owner of the entity on his capital, it is possible to express them in terms of both realized and realizable cash flows (after deduction of the cost of borrowing but before taxation). As above, the denominator of owner's capital ought to be the average of the period in order to provide a meaningful return for the period.

	1980	*1981*	*1982*	*1983*	*1984*	*1985*
	£000	*£000*	*£000*	*£000*	*£000*	*£000*
Average capital employed (m)	66	76	90	104	120	137

The rates of return can now be prepared – in the first case relating to realized cash flow:

	1980	*1981*	*1982*	*1983*	*1984*	*1985*
	%	*%*	*%*	*%*	*%*	*%*
Realized rate of return (n)	6.1	5.3	14.4	16.3	13.3	16.1

The realized return to the owner, therefore, has increased from an approximately 6% in 1980 to more than 16% by 1985. The return is before tax but after the cost of servicing debt, and can be compared with that for equivalent investments. The fuller rate in realizable terms is as follows:

	1980	*1981*	*1982*	*1983*	*1984*	*1985*
	%	*%*	*%*	*%*	*%*	*%*
Realizable rate of return (o)	16.7	35.5	32.2	30.8	32.5	26.3

Rising from nearly 17% in 1980 to more than 30% in the next four years, and falling to 26% in 1985, the realizable rate reflects sale price changes not converted fully into cash flow terms. The analyst can use it either in inter- or intra-firm comparisons.

ASSET MANAGEMENT

The final group of CFR-based indicators concerns the financial position of the entity. In broad terms, this can be examined by comparing the cash or cash-equivalent available to it in the form of realized and readily-realizable assets with its liabilities due for repayment in the short-term. This gives a measure of the potential cash cover for the short-term lenders concerned, and in compatible measurement terms which are relevant to a consideration of such financing matters.

The data required for this purpose in this chapter are contained in the Summarized Statement of Financial Position. By dividing total assets (all readily-realizable in this case) by short-term liabilities (including the bank overdraft, which is technically repayable in the short-term), the overall cover can be derived as follows:

	1980	*1981*	*1982*	*1983*	*1984*	*1985*
Overall liquidity, or cash cover (p)	4.24	3.13	2.60	2.42	2.17	2.01

The above data reveal a steadily deteriorating situation – the short-term liability cover being halved between 1980 and 1985. This may be due to a dimunition of readily-realizable assets and/or an increase in the short-term financing of the entity. In fact, the assets total increased by 222% between 1980 and 1985 (from £89,000 to £287,000), whilst liabilities increased by 581% (from £21,000 to £143,000). This was due largely to the increase of the bank overdraft from £5,000 in 1980 to £65,000 in 1985 – an expansion of 1200%.

Working capital may also be examined in the form of a restricted definition of the term, again using CFR data but limiting the assets and liabilities concerned to those arising from the trading and related activities of the entity. The previous data assumed a comparison of readily-realizable assets with short-term liabilities which, because of the composition of the former, takes a seeming liquidation view of the entity. A narrower interpretation of net assets, akin to that of traditional analysis, looks at those readily-realizable assets that should be available in the normal course of operations to meet short-term liabilities that require to be repaid. Thus, in the example given in Appendix 7, the working capital structure in sale price terms would be:

	1980	*1981*	*1982*	*1983*	*1984*	*1985*
	£000	*£000*	*£000*	*£000*	*£000*	*£000*
Operating assets						
Debtors	20	37	53	71	92	115
Stock	15	27	33	36	58	74
	35	64	86	107	150	189
Short-term liabilities						
Creditors	10	20	23	26	43	57
Taxation	4	8	10	10	14	13
Distribution	2	4	6	7	7	8
	16	32	39	43	64	78

The readily-realizable property and fittings would not be available in the normal course of events for repayment of short-term liabilities, and the latter would not include the bank overdraft unless the bank made a specific decision regarding repayment.

By dividing operating assets by the short-term liabilities, the cash cover in the normal course of operations becomes available:

	1980	*1981*	*1982*	*1983*	*1984*	*1985*
Operating cash cover (q)	2.19	2.00	2.21	2.49	2.34	2.42

With the exclusion of the overdraft from the working capital position, it can be seen that the cash cover has improved slightly but steadily over the six-year period. Once again, however, this comparative review has been made by using CFR data that properly relate available assets to known liabilities – that is in actual or potential cash flow terms.

SUMMARY

The previous sections have produced the following analyses relevant to the use of CFR-based earnings and financial position:

	1980	*1981*	*1982*	*1983*	*1984*	*1985*
	%	%	%	%	%	%
Realized earnings	36	15	45	53	41	61
Unrealized earnings	64	85	55	47	59	39
Realizable earnings	100	100	100	100	100	100
Capital employed	76	68	62	59	54	50
Short-term liabilities	24	32	38	41	46	50
Total assets	100	100	100	100	100	100
Gearing	7	8	18	24	26	31
Entity realized rate of return	6	5	10	12	10	11
Entity realizable rate of return	14	26	22	20	21	16
Equity realized rate of return	6	5	14	16	13	16
Equity realizable rate of return	17	36	32	31	33	26
*Overall liquidity cover**	4.24	3.13	2.60	2.42	2.17	2.01
*Operating cash cover**	2.19	2.00	2.21	2.49	2.34	2.42

* *Absolute, not percentage figures.*

The above data are CFR-based, which makes them internally consistent and comparable. Each datum adds to the analyst's knowledge of the financial performance and position of the reporting entity, and specifically to the combined effect of profitability and liquidity. Other ratios could be added to the above list, but the latter are offered as the basic CFR framework for analysis from which these other ratios can be developed.

CHAPTER 9 Further issues and thoughts

Previous chapters have attempted to outline the main features of, and arguments for, a system of external financial reporting based on a combination of cash flows and sale prices. The measurement, reporting and usage of such information has been explained and discussed in detail, but it would be wrong to imply that such procedures do not involve problems of accounting and disclosure that require further attention and thought. The purpose of this chapter is to outline these problems with a view to further thinking and research taking place. They reveal the not unsurprising conclusion that the CFR system has problems similar in terms of general principle to those of other forms of reporting – that is, measurement, disclosure, usage and feasibility. Each of these areas will be examined in turn.

MEASUREMENT PROBLEMS

CFR attempts to measure what exists or happens at a specific point of time. In this sense, it is not particularly concerned with what has proceeded reported events or what might follow them. It therefore attempts to describe factually the cash flow effects of management actions without recourse to history or forecasting. However, the measurement process is not entirely free from personal judgment (and, arguably, may never be).

(1) There are considerable problems of classification of data in CFR. For example, the various financial statements advocated in this text depend on classifying assets in terms of an order of realizability – from the most to the least realizable. This breaks away from the traditional fixed and current asset categories, and requires the reporting accountant to consider continuously each asset in terms of its sale price – the more definite and available the latter is, the greater the evidence of realizability. This is a matter that should not be legislated for; the accountant must look to the sale price evidence on each reporting occasion to judge the realizability of each asset. The latter should not be regarded as having a permanent classification throughout its existence in the reporting entity.

(2) A similar problem arises with respect to the classification of individual inflows and outflows, and appears to have roots in the long-lived issue of distinguishing between capital and revenue items. In CFR, the most obvious examples relate to the judgment to be made as to whether or

not particular data relate to operational or investment flows. For example, expenditure on research and development, renovation and advertising could be classified as operational rather than investment cash outflows (and thus would diminish realized operating cash flows and not appear in the Statement of Financial Position). Different judgments in this respect obviously could have significant effects on judging the operational viability of the entity in terms of such indicators as returns on capital employed and operating margins.

This is a problem that exists in all forms of external financial reporting, and is therefore not unique to CFR. It could be extended to similar judgments, such as categorizing grants received from government and other like bodies, and receipts from asset sale transactions. Perhaps the solution is to be found in terms of the realizability of the subject-matter concerned. First, in relation to expenditure, if there is evidence of an identifiable resource with a potential market and sale price, it could be argued that this represents an investment that should be treated as a realizable asset. If there is no such evidence, it would appear prudent to treat the item as an operating or trading outflow. Classification of reporting items as assets would then result in any subsequent inflow (for example, a grant or a sale receipt) being matched with it in a consistent fashion. The key issue, however, appears to be realizability.

(3) CFR attempts to avoid time-period allocations of costs that have no real-world referent. On occasion, this has been taken to imply that CFR advocates are suggesting that the system is free from all allocation judgments.[48] This is not the case, as the points in 1 and 2 above illustrate.[49] Classifications are a form of allocation, and require subjective judgments to be applied by the reporting accountant. Other examples could include the vexed problem of distinguishing between ordinary and extraordinary transactions. No matter how many definitions of the latter terms are made, and no matter how many quantitative guidelines are laid down, the issue will always be one for final resolution according to the circumstances of the individual reporting entity. Similarly, if the reporting involves segmented data, the accountant inevitably will be faced with data that do not fit easily or directly into the defined segments. In these situations in CFR, the criterion of correspondence should dominate – if the allocation judgment results in data that do not correspond to the reality of the transactions to which they relate, then the spurious allocation should not be attempted.[50] CFR attempts to avoid these allocations. It cannot be said to ignore them.

(4) CFR depends to a considerable extent on the choice of sale prices by the reporting accountant. The use of sale prices is not a simple issue of going out into the market and identifying the price for a particular asset. There are often many different prices to choose from. For example, prices for the same asset can vary from market to market depending on such matters as location, availability, and the extent of customer demand. A sensible solution would appear to be to use

prices in the market in which the entity typically trades or exchanges.

A further problem is whether to use a sale price that assumes an immediate liquidation and exiting of the asset from the entity[51] or a sale in the normal course of trading (that is, finding a buyer and deducting expenses to get the asset into a reasonable condition for sale).[52] This text takes the latter view of sale prices because it appears to correspond best with the reality of what the entity does with its assets. But others might argue that pure exit prices are the more factual representations of that reality for reporting purposes.

All forms of accounting for external financial reporting involve the so-called aggregation problem in the valuation of assets – that is, different aggregates are achieved when either valuing a group of assets or valuing them singly. Several writers have examined this problem in relation to sale prices,[53] but no definitive solution has been achieved.[54] However, it could be argued that the computed valuation should take into account the usual way in which management would seek to realize the assets concerned – for example, if they are normally sold singly, then aggregates of single values should be determined.

Finally, the problem of the non-vendible asset affects CFR. Assets for which there is no market need not necessarily have no sale price. The difficulties of evidencing the latter is such circumstances would appear to justify the approach based on correspondence – if no sale price is evident, the asset has a zero value and this fact should be reported.[55]

(5) Non-cash transactions are a common feature of accounting, although they may not occur frequently (for example, generally, the acquisition of assets through loans or capital issues; and, specifically, the long-term leasing of assets). Because they do not involve cash flows when initiated, such transactions could be ignored in the CFR system. But important information would then remain undisclosed merely because, in effect, a cash inflow had been cancelled by an equal and opposite cash outflow. Thus, two options are open to the reporting accountant – either to report such quasi-cash transactions separately with a full explanation of the current cash equivalent flows involved;[56] or to treat them as if they were cash flows (for example, in the Statement of Realized Cash Flow, the leased asset could be treated as an investment outflow at the present value of the future lease payments, with the equivalent figure being shown as a borrowing inflow; the asset could then be shown at its zero value in the Statement of Financial Position and the 100% write off would be shown in the Statement of Realizable Earnings). This treatment has the advantage of bringing the items concerned into the financial statements. It avoids the complications of separate disclosure, and reflects the reality of the transactions – the acquisition of assets by borrowing, and the resultant zero sale prices attributable to them. As before, this is a problem that is not unique to CFR, as it applies also to each of the alternative systems of external financial reporting.

DISCLOSURE PROBLEMS

Reporting involves measurement and disclosure, and CFR has its fair share of disclosure problems. As each is applicable to all forms of reporting, their lack of resolution in CFR ought not to invalidate it necessarily.

(1) One of the crucial issues in CFR is the question of terminology. Accounting depends on a complex and, at times, confusing language. The latter lacks unique definitions of key terms, and can provide the basis for serious and incomplete understanding by users.[57] The suggested CFR system would be no stranger to this problem. It involves the use of terminology such as operating cash flow, capital expenditure, realizable earnings, readily- and not-readily-realizable assets, and short and long-term liabilities. To be understandable, these terms should be either defined for users or other terms should be found for and defined in CFR statements.

(2) A further disclosure problem relates to the amount of detail to be disclosed in the CFR system (again, a situation that affects all financial reports). In order that financial statements are relevant, sufficient information should be disclosed to provide a comprehensible surrogate for a direct experience of what is being reported on. However, too much information can cloud or obscure key issues in financial reports. The problem is one of striking an adequate balance between what the entity needs to report and how much explanation is thereby required.[58] In CFR, the issues could involve the degree to which segmented data can be reported sensibly and relevantly (particularly because of the allocation problem), and the extent to which the CFR information needs to be supported by detailed explanation (for example, capital expenditure data being split between replacement and growth investment; and operating cash flows being analysed into their constituent parts). There is no definitive solution to this problem, because so much depends on individual judgments of the reporting entity's circumstances, and the specific needs and expertise of report users.

(3) Earlier suggestions relating to CFR advocated the reporting of forecast data to provide as complete a package of relevant financial information as possible.[59] This text has concentrated on the measurement and disclosure of CFR data ex post on the grounds that CFR is attempting to be as factual as possible. Forecasting introduces totally subjective reports that depend on estimates of events to come. This appears to conflict with many of the arguments made for CFR, and some writers would argue it should not be part of any system of accounting.[60] This is a matter over which considerable debate continues, irrespective of the basis of accounting and reporting. Thus, it is not considered further within the context of a text concerned largely with ex post financial reporting.

(4) It is a generally accepted feature of external financial reporting that the information contained in the published financial statements is

subject to audit by an independent qualified accountant. CFR should be no stranger to this function, which would not alter considerably from that applied to historic cost accounting. The basic principles of auditing will remain, although the emphasis would be on verifying classifications and sale price aggregations rather than traditional time-period cost allocations. CFR-based financial statements ought therefore to be disclosed with a supporting audit opinion.

USE PROBLEMS

The previous chapters relating to the use to be made of CFR reports were based largely on traditional principles of ratio analysis. However, they introduced the reader to matters that create new problems for the financial analyst.

(1) Ideally, CFR data ought to be prepared and reported by business entities. Until such a point is reached, a surrogate approach to analysing realized cash flows can be made by using funds statements. This involves various adjustments to obtain pure cash flow data, and certain assumptions also require to be made in order to complete such a task (for example, the attribution of all working capital items to the trading profit in order to obtain the operating cash flow). In addition, many of the classification problems mentioned above will affect funds statements – for example, the analyst will be relying on the reporting accountant's judgments concerning the classification of expenditure between capital and revenue items.

(2) Many entities are affected by foreign exchange translation problems in their accounting, and exchange differences can seriously affect published financial results. In funds statements, the various inflows and outflows can include a combination of the value of transactions at the time they took place plus or minus any relevant exchange differences since these times – for example, changes in the stated figures for stock, debtors and creditors can include the latter items. Existing guidance on such practices is non-existent, and the CFR analyst therefore will require to eliminate such exchange adjustments in order to reveal the cash flows that pertained at the time of the various transactions. This may be impossible unless the entity makes such eliminations when producing its funds statement or discloses sufficient information for this to be done by the analyst. If these circumstances prevail, the latter person must at least recognise the possibility of his CFR data being distorted by the inclusion of foreign exchange adjustments.

(3) The constraint of a traditional twelve-month reporting period for business entities creates difficulties for the CFR analyst, and, as mentioned earlier, it is recommended that multi-period aggregates could be used. The specific reporting periods to build into the series are a matter of analytical judgement, dependent on the expertise and

knowledge of the entity held by the analyst. There is little that can be legislated for in this area. In any case it is not an issue that affects only the reporting of CFR data (all external reporting systems suffer from the same inherent problem).

THE FEASIBILITY OF THE CFR SYSTEM

Questions will inevitably arise regarding the feasibility of the suggestions made in this text, particularly regarding the availability of sale price data.[61] Assuming the system is generally acceptable, then the possibility of not obtaining sale prices for particular assets arises. However, in these circumstances, it is argued that, if no sale price is available, this would be evidence of the non-realizability of the asset, and an indication of the degree of financial risk that the entity was accepting by holding it. In other words, the factual nature of CFR, and its adherence to the criterion of correspondence, causes the problem of sale prices to be less acute than might appear at first.

In any case, there is considerable evidence of CFR applications in traditional financial reporting – for example, funds statement practices involve a considerable use of cash flow data; historic cost accounting applies the lower of cost or market rule, with market interpreted usually in terms of sale prices; the value to owner rule utilized in current cost accounting involves a comparative use of sale prices; and companies utilize sale prices when occasionally revaluing properties, disclosing valuations for listed securities, and providing for bad debts. The financial reporter is therefore no stranger to cash flows and sale prices.

CONCLUSIONS

This text has been concerned to advocate the case for CFR, and to demonstrate its form and usage. Without rehearsing the various arguments already made in this and previous chapters, the following major conclusions may be made.

(1) CFR is a system that emphasizes the importance of each of the key accounting criteria – that is, CFR information is relevant to many user groups and therefore has a general-purpose quality; it reflects the activities of the reporting entity as factually as possible; it does not involve complex measurement procedures; it can be used to reflect time periods that involve company activity unconstrained by the traditional form of annual reporting; and it requires support from detailed disclosures to provide adequate comprehension in much the same way as traditional reporting.

(2) It appears to avoid many, but not all, of the problems of traditional accounting, and those that remain are of a type that accountants have long found bearable.

(3) If required, it can be used as a complete system of reporting or, alternatively, it may be used in conjunction with other forms of reporting. Whichever approach is adopted, CFR attempts to reflect the key financial consideration in business – the availability of cash flow to the entity.

Appendix 1

Year to 31 December 1979	*Property*	*Plant and machinery*	*Motor vehicles*	*Finished goods*	*Work-in-progress*	*Debtors*	*Bank*	*Creditors*	*Taxation*	*Distributions*	*Loan*	*Capital*	*Retained earnings*
	£000	*£000*	*£000*	*£000*	*£000*	*£000*	*£000*	*£000*	*£000*	*£000*	*£000*	*£000*	*£000*
Opening position	20	6	4	18	24	18	44	(18)	(20)	(12)	(18)	(10)	(56)
Credit sales						213							(213)
Cash from customers						(210)	210						
Credit purchases, wages, etc.					137			(137)					
Cash to suppliers, employees							(136)	136					
Cost of goods manufactured*				132	(132)								
Cost of goods sold†				(128)									128
Interest paid							(3)						3
Tax provided									(17)				17
Tax paid							(20)		20				
Distribution provided										(25)			25
Distribution paid							(12)			12			
Capital expenditure		34	20				(54)						
Sale price adjustments‡	7	(18)	(7)	3	(1)								16
Closing position	27	22	17	25	28	21	29	(19)	(17)	(25)	(18)	(10)	(80)

* Required in order to obtain the historic cost of goods sold.
† Required in order to obtain a measure of historic cost profit for purposes, say, of taxation.
‡ Balancing figures required to produce the period-end asset data in sale price terms. These figures partly reflect changes in sale price, and partly adjustments to cater for a mixture of historic costs and sale prices.

Appendix 2

Year to 31 December 1980	*Property*	*Plant and machinery*	*Motor vehicles*	*Finished goods*	*Work-in-progress*	*Debtors*	*Bank*	*Creditors*	*Taxation*	*Distributions*	*Loan*	*Capital*	*Retained earnings*
	£000	*£000*	*£000*	*£000*	*£000*	*£000*	*£000*	*£000*	*£000*	*£000*	*£000*	*£000*	*£000*
Opening position	27	22	17	25	28	21	29	(19)	(17)	(25)	(18)	(10)	(80)
Credit sales						237							(237)
Cash from customers						(232)	232						
Credit purchases, wages, etc.					180			(180)					
Cash to suppliers, employees							(172)	172					
Cost of goods manufactured*				171	(171)								
Cost of goods sold†				(166)									166
Interest paid							(3)						3
Tax provided									(18)				18
Tax paid							(17)		17				
Distribution provided										(30)			30
Distribution paid							(25)			25			
Capital expenditure		11					(11)						
Sale price adjustments‡	4	(13)	(6)	—	(1)								16
Closing position	31	20	11	30	36	26	33	(27)	(18)	(30)	(18)	(10)	(84)

* Required in order to obtain the historic cost of goods sold.

† Required in order to obtain a measure of historic cost profit for purposes, say, of taxation.

‡ Balancing figures required to produce the period-end asset data in sale price terms. These figures partly reflect changes in sale price, and partly adjustments to cater for a mixture of historic costs and sale prices.

Appendix 3

Year to 31 December 1981	*Property*	*Plant and machinery*	*Motor vehicles*	*Finished goods*	*Work-in-progress*	*Debtors*	*Bank*	*Creditors*	*Taxation*	*Distributions*	*Loan*	*Capital*	*Retained earnings*
	£000	*£000*	*£000*	*£000*	*£000*	*£000*	*£000*	*£000*	*£000*	*£000*	*£000*	*£000*	*£000*
Opening position	31	20	11	30	36	26	33	(27)	(18)	(30)	(18)	(10)	(84)
Credit sales						249							(249)
Cash from customers						(238)	238						
Credit purchases, wages, etc.					185			(185)					
Cash to suppliers, employees							(185)	185					
Cost of goods manufactured*				183	(183)								
Cost of goods sold†				(179)									179
Interest paid							(3)						3
Tax provided									(16)				16
Tax paid							(18)		18				
Distribution provided										(30)			30
Distribution paid							(30)			30			
Capital expenditure		17					(17)						
Sale price adjustments‡	2	(14)	(6)	1	(3)								20
Closing position	33	23	5	35	35	37	18	(27)	(16)	(30)	(18)	(10)	(85)

* Required in order to obtain the historic cost of goods sold.

† Required in order to obtain a measure of historic cost profit for purposes, say, of taxation.

‡ Balancing figures required to produce the period-end asset data in sale price terms. These figures partly reflect changes in sale price, and partly adjustments to cater for a mixture of historic costs and sale prices.

Appendix 4

	Property	Plant and machinery	Motor vehicles	Finished goods	Work-in-progress	Debtors	Bank	Creditors	Taxation	Distributions	Loan	Capital	Retained earnings
	£000	£000	£000	£000	£000	£000	£000	£000	£000	£000	£000	£000	£000
Opening position	33	23	5	35	35	37	18	(27)	(16)	(30)	(18)	(10)	(85)
Credit sales						264							(264)
Cash from customers						(261)	261						
Credit purchases, wages, etc.					214			(214)					
Cash to suppliers, employees							(211)	211					
Cost of goods manufactured*				205	(205)								
Cost of goods sold†				(200)									200
Interest paid							(4)						4
Tax provided									(17)				17
Tax paid							(16)		16				
Distribution provided										(25)			25
Distribution paid							(30			30			
Capital expenditure		7	15				(22)						
Loan received							4				(4)		
Sale price adjustments‡	6	(9)	(7)	—	(2)								12
Closing position	39	21	13	40	42	40	—	(30)	(17)	(25)	(22)	(10)	(91)

* Required in order to obtain the historic cost of goods sold.
† Required in order to obtain a measure of historic cost profit for purposes, say, of taxation.
‡ Balancing figures required to produce the period-end asset data in sale price terms. These figures partly reflect changes in sale price, and partly adjustments to cater for a mixture of historic costs and sale prices.

Appendix 5

	Stables and offices	*Stage coaches*	*Horses*	*Stock of feedstuffs*	*Bank*	*Creditors*	*Distribution*	*Capital*	*Retained earnings*
	£000	*£000*	*£000*	*£000*	*£000*	*£000*	*£000*	*£000*	*£000*
Position 31.12.77	20	42	21	3	7	(7)	(6)	(10)	(70)
Cash sales					209				(209)
Credit purchases, wages, etc.*				204		(204)			
Cash to suppliers, employees					(204)	204			
Cost of sales*				(203)					203
Distribution provided							(5)		5
Distribution paid					(6)		6		
Sale price adjustments	(5)	(12)	(3)						20
Position 31.12.78	15	30	18	4	6	(7)	(5)	(10)	(51)
Cash sales					157				(157)
Credit purchases, wages, etc.*				144		(144)			
Cash to suppliers, employees					(145)	145			
Cost of sales*				(143)					143
Distribution provided							(5)		5
Distribution paid					(5)		5		
Capital expenditure			5		(5)				
Sale price adjustments	(5)	(16)	(4)						25
Position 31.12.79	10	14	19	5	8	(6)	(5)	(10)	(35)

Cash sales					136				(136)
Credit purchases, wages, etc.*				131		(131)			
Cash to suppliers, employees					(132)	132			
Cost of sales*				(131)					131
Distribution provided							(4)		4
Distribution paid					(5)		5		
Capital expenditure			3		(3)				
Sale price adjustments		(6)	(2)						8
Position 31.12.80	10	8	20	5	4	(5)	(4)	(10)	(28)
Cash sales					91				(91)
Credit purchases, wages, etc.*				88		(88)			
Cash to suppliers, employees					(87)	87			
Cost of sales*				(87)					87
Distribution provided							(4)		4
Distribution paid					(4)		4		
Sale price adjustments		(4)	(4)						8
Position 31.12.81	10	4	16	6	4	(6)	(4)	(10	(20)
Cash sales					38				(38)
Credit purchases, wages, etc.*				35		(35)			
Cash to suppliers, employees					(36)	36			
Cost of sales*				(35)					35
Distribution provided							(4)		4
Distribution paid					(4)		4		
Sale price adjustments		(3)	(1)						4
Position 31.12.82	10	1	15	6	2	(5)	(4)	(10)	(15)

* For convenience, all operating expenditure has been dealt with through the stock account. Owing to the lower of cost or market rule, stock has been accounted for on a historic cost basis at its sale price. The question of taxation has been ignored throughout.

Appendix 6

PROFIT STATEMENTS

	1980	*1981*	*1982*	*1983*	*1984*	*1985*
	£000	*£000*	*£000*	*£000*	*£000*	*£000*
Sales	84	130	206	237	299	410
Less: cost of sales (1)	64	99	157	181	236	329
	20	31	49	56	63	81
Less: other expenses	7	10	18	21	25	36
	13	21	31	35	38	45
Less: depreciation of fittings	5	5	8	11	13	13
	8	16	23	24	25	32
Less: taxation provided	4	8	10	10	14	13
	4	8	13	14	11	19
Less: dividends provided	2	4	6	7	7	8
Retained profits	2	4	7	7	4	11

BALANCE SHEETS

	1979	*1980*	*1981*	*1982*	*1983*	*1984*	*1985*
	£000	*£000*	*£000*	*£000*	*£000*	*£000*	*£000*
Property (2)	31	31	50	50	50	70	70
Fittings (3)	25	20	15	22	26	23	30
Stock (4)	10	12	22	27	30	48	62
Debtors	12	20	37	53	71	92	115
Bank	(5)	(5)	(7)	(21)	(35)	(46)	(65)
Creditors	(9)	(10)	(20)	(23)	(26)	(43)	(57)
Taxation	(2)	(4)	(8)	(10)	(10)	(14)	(13)
Dividends	(2)	(2)	(4)	(6)	(7)	(7)	(8)
	60	62	85	92	99	123	134
Capital	50	50	50	50	50	50	50
Reserve (5)	—	—	19	19	19	39	39
Retained profits	10	12	16	23	30	34	45
	60	62	85	92	99	123	134

(1) Purchase of goods adjusted for opening and closing stock.
(2) No depreciation provided; increases due to revaluation.
(3) At cost less depreciation aggregate.
(4) At cost.
(5) Revaluation of property surpluses.

Appendix 7

STATEMENTS OF REALIZABLE EARNINGS (Year to 31 December)

	1980 £000	1981 £000	1982 £000	1983 £000	1984 £000	1985 £000
Realized earnings						
Operating cash flow	4	4	13	17	16	22
Realizable earnings						
Readily-realizable net assets:						
Debtors	8	17	16	18	21	23
Stock	3	12	6	3	22	16
Property	4	7	4	8	8	6
Fittings	(7)	(3)	(7)	(11)	(11)	(17)
(Creditors)	(1)	(10)	(3)	(3)	(17)	(14)
	7	23	16	15	23	14
	11	27	29	32	39	36
Less: taxation provided	4	8	10	10	14	13
	7	19	19	22	25	23
Less: capital maintenance adjustment*	3	5	6	4	10	10
	4	14	13	18	15	13
Less: distribution provided	2	4	6	7	7	8
	2	10	7	11	8	5
Add: retained earnings of prior periods	10	12	22	29	40	48
Retained earnings carried forward	12	22	29	40	48	53

* Assuming period-end general index points as follows:

1979	1980	1981	1982	1983	1984	1985
129	136	146	157	163	178	192

The adjustments are:

1980 = £63,000 × $^{136}/_{129}$ − 63,000

1981 = £68,000 × $^{146}/_{136}$ − 68,000

1982 = £83,00 × 157/146 − 83,000
1983 = £96,000 × 163/157 − 36,000
1984 = £111,000 × 178/163 − 111,000
1985 = £129,000 × 192/178 − 129,000

STATEMENTS OF FINANCIAL POSITION (as at 31 December)

	1979	*1980*	*1981*	*1982*	*1983*	*1984*	*1985*
	£000	*£000*	*£000*	*£000*	*£000*	*£000*	*£000*
Readily-realizable assets							
Debtors	12	20	37	53	71	92	115
Stock	12	15	27	33	36	58	74
Property	39	43	50	54	62	70	76
Fittings	18	11	8	16	20	19	22
	81	89	122	156	189	239	287
Less: short-term liabilities							
Bank	5	5	7	21	35	46	65
Creditors	9	10	20	23	26	43	57
Taxation	2	4	8	10	10	14	13
Distribution	2	2	4	6	7	7	8
	18	21	39	60	78	110	143
	63	68	83	96	111	129	144
	63	68	83	96	111	129	144
Owner's equity							
Capital	50	50	50	50	50	50	50
Capital maintenance reserve	3	6	11	17	21	31	41
Retained earnings	10	12	22	29	40	48	53
	63	68	83	96	111	129	144

Footnotes and references

1. When dealing with conventional accounting practice, the term 'funds statement' will be used throughout this text in preference to the alternatives of 'sources and application of funds statement' or 'statement of changes in financial position'. The latter term will be used, however, when describing cash flow-based funds statements in Chapter 5 onwards.
2. Each of these fundamental aspects of accounting have formed part of major studies related to the structure of the financial reporting function – for example, Accounting Objectives Study Group, *Objectives of Financial Statements*, American Institute of Certified Public Accountants, 1973; Accounting Standards Committee, *The Corporate Report*, 1975; Committee to Prepare a Statement of Basic Accounting Theory, *A Statement of Basic Accounting Theory*, 1966; and Inflation Accounting Committee, 'Inflation Accounting,' *Report of the Inflation Accounting Committee*, HMSO, 1975.
3. This fundamental of accounting can be attributed to R.J. Chambers, *Accounting, Evaluation and Economic Behaviour*, Prentice-Hall, 1966, passim. It has also been used within the context of the external audit function – see T.A. Lee, *Company Auditing*, Gee, 1982, passim.
4. The potential for confusing allocated historic costs and sale prices is seen in evidence in D.P. Tweedie, 'Cash Flows and Realizable Values: the Intuitive Accounting Concepts? An Empirical Test,' *Accounting and Business Research*, Winter 1977, pp. 2–17.
5. For detailed review of the issue of predictive ability, see K.V. Peasnell, 'The Usefulness of Accounting Information to Investors,' *ICRA Occasional Paper 1*, University of Lancaster, 1973. It is not the purpose of this text to pursue the issue of predictive ability in relation to cash flows, but, obviously, it is a topic that will require further empirical investigation.
6. It is difficult to define the term 'performance' with any degree of precision, and it is used in this text to describe the effectiveness of managerial activities conducted in order to meet prescribed financial objectives.
7. This approach owes its origins to discussions of Hicks in relation to guidelines for personal economic behaviour – see, for example, J.R. Hicks, *Value and Capital*, Clarendon Press, 1946, pp. 171–81.
8. There is a continuing debate as to whether assets should be regarded as tangible (and intangible) resources in the possession of the reporting entity (the usual accounting approach) or representations of future benefits in the form of cash flows (the contemporary economic approach). For purposes of this text, a variation of the economic approach is adopted.
9. For a fuller discussion of all these issues, see T.A. Lee, *Income and Value Measurement: Theory and Practice*, Van Nostrand, 1980.
10. The system could also be described in terms of second-hand replacement costs, but it is doubtful whether entity management would consider such replacements

in practice. Nevertheless, there has been support for such reporting – see E. Stamp, 'Financial Reports on an Entity: Ex Uno Plures,' in R.R. Sterling and A.L. Thomas (eds.), *Accounting for a Simplified Firm Owning Depreciable Assets*, Scholars Book Co., 1979, pp. 175–6.

11. The issue of the nature of accounting capital, and how to account and report on it, has been pursued in considerable depth in K.W. Lemke and R.R. Sterling (eds.), *Maintenance of Capital – Financial Versus Physical*, Scholars Book Co., 1982.
12. For the origins of such an interpretation of capital, see R.J. Chambers, *Accounting, Evaluation and Economic Behaviour*, Prentice-Hall, 1966, pp. 114–5.
13. Argued for in detail in L. Revsine, 'Physical Capital Maintenance: An Analysis,' in K.W. Lemke and R.R. Sterling (eds.), *Maintenance of Capital – Financial Versus Physical*, Scholars Book Co., 1982, pp. 75–94.
14. For a general discussion of holding gains, see T.A. Lee, *Income and Value Measurement: Theory and Practice*, Van Nostrand, 1982, p. 85–8; and P. Prakash and S. Sunder, 'The Case Against Separation of Current Operating Profit and Holding Gain,' *The Accounting Review*, January 1979, pp. 1–22.
15. For a discussion of backlog depreciation, see Inflation Accounting Committee, 'Inflation Accounting,' *Report of the Inflation Accounting Committee*, HMSO, 1975, pp. 142–6.
16. There is, however, a growing body of evidence of user needs and user behaviour – for example, H.K. Baker and J.A. Haslem, 'Information Needs of Individual Investors,' *Journal of Accountancy*, November 1973, pp. 64–9; J.J. Benjamin and K.G. Stanga, 'Differences in Disclosure Needs of Major Users of Financial Statements, *Accounting and Business Research*, Summer 1977, pp. 187–92; R.H. Chenhall and R. Juchau, 'Investor Information Needs – An Australian Study,' *Accounting and Business Research*, Spring 1977, pp. 111–19; T.A. Lee and D.P. Tweedie, 'Accounting Information: An Investigation of Shareholder Usage,' *Accounting and Business Research*, Autumn 1975, pp. 280–91: T.A. Lee and D.P. Tweedie, *The Private Shareholder and the Corporate Report*, Institute of Chartered Accountants in England and Wales, 1977, pp. 52–77; and T.A. Lee and D.P. Tweedie, *The Institutional Investor and Financial Information*, Institute of Chartered Accountants in England and Wales, 1981, pp. 65–103.
17. See, for example, T.A. Lee and D.P. Tweedie, 'Accounting Information: An Investigation of Shareholder Understanding,' *Accounting and Business Research*, Winter 1975, pp. 3–17; T.A. Lee and D.P. Tweedie, *The Private Shareholder and the Corporate Report*, Institute of Chartered Accountants in England and Wales, 1977, pp. 27–51; and T.A. Lee and D.P. Tweedie, *The Institutional Investor and Financial Information*, Institute of Chartered Accountants in England and Wales, 1981, pp. 30–64.
18. A point long argued by Chambers – for example, in R.J. Chambers, *Accounting, Evaluation and Economic Behaviour*, Prentice-Hall, 1966, passim.
19. For evidence of this point, see D.P. Tweedie, 'Cash Flows and Realizable Values: the Intuitive Accounting Concepts? An Empirical Test,' *Accounting and Business Research*, Winter 1977, pp. 2–177.
20. For a fuller discussion, see R.R. Sterling, 'Conservatism: The Fundamental Principle of Valuation in Traditional Accounting,' *Abacus*, December 1967, pp. 109–32.
21. Stock has to be counted, costed and the 'lower of cost or market' rule applied; debtors have to be judged for realizability; and creditors may include estimated accruals rather than contracted liabilities.

22. These figures have been derived from a comparison of equivalent data in the historic cost and replacement cost balance sheets.
23. A point apparently ignored by writers such as E. Stamp, 'Multi-Column Reporting,' in T.A. Lee (ed.), *Developments in Financial Reporting*, Philip Allan, 1981, pp. 57–77.
24. Evidence of comprehension problems can be found in T.A. Lee and D.P. Tweedie, *The Private Shareholder and the Corporate Report*, Institute of Chartered Accountants in England and Wales, 1977, pp. 33–42; and T.A. Lee and D.P. Tweedie, *The Institutional Investor and Financial Information*, Institute of Chartered Accountants in England and Wales, 1981, pp. 35–44.
25. For example, H.K. Baker and J.A. Haslem, 'Information Needs of Individual Investors,' *Journal of Accountancy*, November 1973, pp. 64–9.
26. As specified, for example, by R.J. Chambers, *Accounting, Evaluation and Economic Behaviour*, Prentice-Hall, 1966; and R.R. Sterling, *Theory of the Measurement of Enterprise Income*, University of Kansas Press, 1970.
27. For details of the major contributors to this area, see T.A. Lee, 'Cash Flow Accounting and Corporate Financial Reporting,' in M. Bromwich and A. Hopwood (eds.), *Essays in British Accounting Research*, Pitman, 1981, pp. 63–78.
28. See T.A. Lee, 'Reporting Cash Flows and Net Realizable Values,' *Accounting and Business Research*, Spring 1981, pp. 163–70.
29. It should also be noted that Heath has examined the issue of asset and liability classification (including realization and payability). He concluded that the present ordering should continue with no classifications and increased supplementary disclosure (L.C. Heath, 'Financial Reporting and the Evaluation of Solvency', *Accounting Research Monograph 3*, American Institute of Certified Public Accountants, 1978, pp. 71–86).
30. This view is compatible with R.J. Chambers, *Accounting, Evaluation and Economic Behaviour*, Prentice Hall, 1966, pp. 202–4; and opposite to that of R.R. Sterling, *Towards a Science of Accounting*, Scholars Book Co., 1979, p. 220, who regards immediate liquidation prices as being the most relevant for reporting purposes. There are thus differences even within the same school of thought.
31. This view is given as a deliberate attempt to be compatible with the positions of Chambers and Sterling despite their use of different forms of sale price.
32. A similar, if differently prescribed statement, has been recommended in L.C. Heath, 'Financial Reporting and the Evaluation of Solvency', *Accounting Research Monograph 3*, American Institute of Certified Public Accountants, 1978, pp. 109–35 (together with other statements concerning the financing and investment activities of the reporting entity).
33. See T.A. Lee, *Income and Value Measurement: Theory and Practice*, Van Nostrand, 1980, pp. 139–57, for explanations of generalised purchasing power adjustments.
34. Chambers' system is explained in T.A. Lee, *Income and Value Measurement: Theory and Practice*, Van Nostrand, 1980, pp. 150–51.
35. As suggested in R.J. Chambers, *Accounting, Evaluation and Economic Behaviour*, Prentice Hall, 1966, pp. 108–9; and implemented in T.A. Lee, 'Reporting Cash Flows and Net Realizable Values,' *Accounting and Business Research*, Spring 1981, pp. 163–70.
36. An approach advocated in R.J. Chambers, 'Accounting for Inflation,' *Exposure Draft*, University of Sydney, 1975.
37. This is a matter to which no attention was paid in R.J. Chambers, 'Accounting for Inflation,' *Exposure Draft*, University of Sydney, 1975.

38. For example, Accounting Objectives Study Group, *Objectives of Financial Statements*, American Institute of Certified Public Accountants, 1975, passim.
39. This should not be taken to imply that an accounting for cash flows is free from subjective judgments and potential distortions – for example, cash outflows require to be separated and classified.
40. Again, it should be noted that the cash flow system requires considerable judgments to be made regarding such recoveries.
41. As argued, for example, in R.J. Chambers, *Accounting, Evaluation and Economic Behaviour*, Prentice-Hall, 1966, p. 92.
42. For fuller expositions of this topic, see T.A. Lee, 'Utility and Relevance: the Search for Reliable Accounting Information,' *Accounting and Business Research*, Summer 1971, pp. 242–9.
43. A point argued in T.A. Lee, 'The Simplicity and the Complexity of Accounting,' in R.R. Sterling and A.L. Thomas, *Accounting for a Simplified Firm Owning Depreciable Assets*, Scholars Book Co., 1979, pp. 35–55.
44. D.P. Tweedie, 'Cash Flows and Realizable Values: the Intuitive Accounting Concepts? An Empirical Test,' *Accounting and Business Research*, Winter 1977, pp. 2–17.
45. See T.A. Lee, 'The Accounting Entity Concept, Accounting Standards, and Inflation Accounting,' *Accounting and Business Research*, Spring 1980, pp. 176–86.
46. This matter is something that cannot be prescribed. It must depend on the nature of the entity and its operations, and the awareness of the analyst with regard to the latter features.
47. In this respect, skill is not a feature only of institutional experts. It can also be found amongst groups of non-experts: see, T.A. Lee and D.P. Tweedie, *The Private Shareholder and the Corporate Report*, Institute of Chartered Accountants in England and Wales, 1977, passim.
48. For example, B.A. Rutherford, 'The Interpretation of Cash Flow Reports and the Other Allocation Problem,' *Abacus*, June 1982, pp. 40–9.
49. And as argued in T.A. Lee, 'Cash Flow Accounting and the Allocation Problem,' *Journal of Business Finance and Accounting*, Autumn 1982, pp. 341–52.
50. As argued in T.A. Lee, 'Cash Flow Accounting and the Allocation Problem,' *Journal of Business Finance and Accounting*,' Autumn 1982, pp. 341–52.
51. R.R. Sterling, *Towards a Science of Accounting*, Scholars Book Co., 1979, p. 220.
52. R.J. Chambers, '*Accounting, Evaluation and Economic Behaviour*, Prentice-Hall, 1966, pp. 202–4.
53. A.L. Thomas, 'The Allocation Problem – Part Two,' *Studies in Accounting Research* 9, American Accounting Association, 1974.
54. R.R. Sterling, *Towards a Science of Accounting*, Scholars Book Co., 1979, p. 172.
55. R.R. Sterling, *Towards a Science of Accounting*, Scholars Book Co., 1979, p. 220.
56. T.A. Lee, 'A Case for Cash Flow Reporting,' *Journal of Business Finance*, Summer 1972, pp. 27–36.
57. As demonstrated in T.A. Lee and D.P. Tweedie, *The Private Shareholder and the Corporate Report*, Institute of Chartered Accountants in England and Wales, 1977, pp. 27–42; and T.A. Lee and D.P. Tweedie, *The Institutional Investor and Financial Information*, Institute of Chartered Accountants in England and Wales, 1981, pp. 30–44.
58. The cry for simplicity in financial reporting is increasing but, if taken at face

value, could provide solutions involving the loss of a considerable amount of relevant financial information. See A.E. Hammill, *Simplified Financial Statements*, Accounting Standards Committee, 1979.

59. See T.A. Lee, 'A Case for Cash Flow Reporting,' *Journal of Business Finance*, Summer 1972, pp. 27–36; and T.A. Lee, 'Reporting Cash Flows and Net Realizable Values,' *Accountancy and Business Economics*, 1981, pp. 82–100.
60. R.J. Chambers, *Accounting, Evaluation and Economic Behaviour*, Prentice-Hall, 1966, pp. 83–4 and 96–9.
61. It is assumed that ex post measurements of cash flows ought not to be a problem.

Bibliography

This text has been written on the basis of much teaching and writing over the years. The following items represent the main contributions by the author to the development of CFR-based systems.

1. 'Goodwill – An Example of Will-O-the-Wisp Accounting,' *Accounting and Business Research*, Autumn 1971, pp. 318–28.
2. 'The Relevance of Accounting Information Including Cash Flows,' *The Accountant's Magazine*, January 1972, pp. 30–34.
3. 'The Nature and Purpose of Cash Flow Reporting,' *The Accountant's Magazine*, April 1972, pp. 198–200 (reproduced in *The South African Chartered Accountant*, November 1972, pp. 429–31).
4. 'A Case for Cash Flow Reporting,' *Journal of Business Finance*, Summer 1972, pp. 27–36 (reproduced in D.A.R. Forester (ed.), *With Disclosed Intent*, Strathclyde Convergencies, 1980, pp. 6–1 to 6–10).
5. 'Enterprise Income: Survival or Decline and Fall?' *Accounting and Business Research*, Summer 1974, pp. 178–92 (reproduced in N.V. Anthony *et al* (eds.), *Readings in Advanced Financial Accounting*, Butterworths (Australia), 1979, pp. 132–46; and in R.H. Parker (ed.), *Readings in Accounting and Business Research 1970–77*, Institute of Chartered Accountants in England and Wales, 1979, pp. 46–60).
6. 'The Cash Flow Accounting Alternative for Corporate Financial Reporting,' in C. van Dam (ed.), *Trends in Managerial and Financial Accounting*, Vol. 1, Martinus Nijhoff, 1978, pp. 63–84.
7. 'The Simplicity and the Complexity of Accounting,' in R.R. Sterling and A.L. Thomas (eds.), *Accounting for a Simplified Firm Owning Depreciable Assets*, Scholars Book Co., 1979, pp. 35–55 (reproduced in T.A. Lee (ed.), *Professors of Accounting at the University of Edinburgh: A Selection of Writings 1919–1983*, University of Edinburgh, 1983).
8. 'The Contribution of Fisher to Cash Flow Accounting – A Resolution of the Accounting Entity Dilemma,' *Journal of Business Finance and Accounting*, Autumn 1979, pp. 321–30.
9. 'Cash Flow Accounting and Corporate Financial Reporting,' in M. Bromwich and A. Hopwood (eds.), *Essays in British Accounting Research*, Pitman, 1981, pp. 63–78.
10. 'Reporting Cash Flows and Net Realizable Values,' *Accounting and Business Research*, Spring 1981 (reproduced in G.W. Dean and M.C. Wells (eds.), *Forerunners of Realizable Value Accounting*, Garland Press, 1983, pp. 313–20).
11. 'Reporting Cash Flows and Net Realizable Values,' *Accountancy and Business Economics* (Netherlands), pp. 82–100 (reproduced in B. Hicks and P. Hunt (eds.), *Cash Flow Accounting*, Laurentian University, 1981, pp. 227–49).
12. 'Cash Flow Accounting and Reporting,' in T.A. Lee (ed.), *Developments in*

Financial Reporting, Philip Allan, 1981, pp. 148–70.
13. 'Support for Cash Flow Accounting,' *The Accountant's Magazine*, May 1981, pp. 146 and 162.
14. 'What Cash Flow Analysis Says About BL's Finances,' *The Financial Times*, 23 October 1981, p. 15.
15. 'A Survey of Accountants' Opinions on Cash Flow Reporting,' *Abacus*, December 1981, pp. 130–44.
16. 'Laker Airways – The Cash Flow Truth,' *Accountancy*, June 1982, pp. 115–16.
17. 'Cash Flow Accounting and the Allocation Problem,' *Journal of Business Finance and Accounting*, Autumn 1982, pp. 341–52.
18. 'A Note on Users and Uses of Cash Flow Information,' *Accounting and Business Research*, Spring 1983, pp. 103–6.
19. 'The Financial Statements and Cash Flow of the Hongkong and Shanghai Banking Corporation: 1865 to 1980,' in F.H.H. King (ed.), *Eastern Banking: Essays in the History of The Hongkong and Shanghai Banking Corporation*, Athlone Press, 1983, pp. 77–92.
20. 'Lonrho: Cash Flows and Borrowing,' *The Accountant*, 19 May 1983, pp. 11–12.
21. 'Funds Statements and Cash Flow Analysis,' *The Investment Analyst*, July 1983, pp. 13–21 (reproduced in *The Accountant's Record*, June/July 1983, pp. 20–7).
22. (with A.W. Stark) 'A Cash Flow Disclosure of Government-Supported Enterprises' Results,' *Journal of Business Finance and Accounting*, Spring 1984, pp. 1–12.
23. 'Towards a Practice of Cash Flow Analysis,' *Paper*, European Accounting Associaton Annual Conference, 1983.

The following additional writings reflect the many and varied contributions made by writers throughout the world to cash flow accounting matters.

A.J. Arnold and B.J. Webb, 'Cash, Profits and Pergamon', *The Accountant*, 8 July 1982, pp. 68–70.

E.V. Artto, *Profitability and Cash Stream Analysis*, Helsinki School of Economics, 1981.

E.V. Artto, 'Replacement Investments, Behaviour of Cash Streams and Income Measurement', in B.E. Hicks and P. Hunt (eds.), *Cash Flow Accounting*, Laurentian University, 1981, pp. 147–62.

R. Ashton, 'Cash Flow Accounting: A Review and Critique', *Journal of Business Finance and Accounting*, Winter 1976, pp. 63–81.

A. Belkaoui, 'Accrual Accounting and Cash Accounting: Relative Merits of Derived Accounting Indicator Numbers', *Journal of Business Finance and Accounting*, Spring 1983, pp. 299–312.

R.S. Clark, 'Statement of Changes: In Need of Change?', *CA Magazine*, February 1983, pp. 26–30.

T.A. Climo, 'Cash Flow Statements for Investors', *Journal of Business Finance and Accounting*, Autumn 1976, pp. 3–14.

J.W. Coughlan, 'Contrast Between Financial-Statement and Discounted-Cash-Flow Methods of Comparing Projects', *NAA Bulletin*, June 1960, pp. 5–17.

J.W. Coughlan, 'Accounting and Capital Budgeting', *The Business Quarterly*, Fall 1962, pp. 39–48.

J.W. Coughlan, 'Funds and Income', *NAA Bulletin*, September 1964, pp. 23–34.

H.C. Edey, 'Accounting Principles and Business Reality', *Accountancy*, November

1963, pp. 998–1002; December 1963, pp. 1083–8.

H.C. Edey, 'The Nature of Profit', *Accounting and Business Research*, Winter 1970, pp. 50–5.

H.B. Ernst, 'New Balance Sheet for Managing Liquidity and Growth', *Harvard Business Review*, March-April 1984, pp. 122–36.

W.L. Ferrara, 'Decision Models, Financial Reporting and Cash Flows', in B.E. Hicks and P. Hunt (eds.), *Cash Flow Accounting*, Laurentian University, 1981, pp. 94–105.

Financial Accounting Standards Board, 'Reporting Funds Flows, Liquidity, and Financial Flexibility', *Discussion Memorandum*, 1980.

M.J. Gombola and J.E. Ketz, 'Similarities Among Asset Flow Measures' in B.E. Hicks and P. Hunt (eds.), *Cash Flow Accounting*, Laurentian University, 1981, pp. 106–24.

M.J. Gombola and J.E. Ketz, 'A Note on Cash Flow and Classification Patterns of Financial Ratios', *The Accounting Review*, January 1983, pp. 105–14.

L.C. Heath, 'Financial Reporting and the Evaluation of Solvency', *Accounting Research Monograph 3*, American Institute of Certified Public Accountants, 1978.

L.C. Heath, 'Cash Receipts and Payments vs Income Reconciliation', in B.E. Hicks and P. Hunt (eds.), *Cash Flow Accounting*, Laurentian University, 1981, pp. 164–71.

B.E. Hicks, 'The Cash Flow Basis of Accounting', in B.E. Hicks and P. Hunt (eds.), *Cash Flow Accounting*, Laurentian University, 1981, pp. 26–39.

P. Hunt, 'A Cure for the Dysfunction of the Funds Statement', in B.E. Hicks and P. Hunt (eds.), *Cash Flow Accounting*, Laurentian University, 1981, pp. 81–92.

Y. Ijiri, 'Cash Flow Accounting and Its Structure', *Journal of Accounting, Auditing and Finance*, May 1978, pp. 331–48.

Y. Ijiri, 'A Simple System of Cash Flow Accounting', in R.R. Sterling and A.L. Thomas (eds.), *Accounting for a Simplified Firm*, Scholars Book Co., 1979, pp. 57–71.

Y. Ijiri, 'Recovery Rate and Cash Flow Accounting', *Financial Executive*, March 1980, pp. 54–60.

Y. Ijiri, 'Historical Cost Accounting and Its Rationality', *Research Monograph 1*, Canadian Certified General Accountants' Research Foundation, 1981, pp. 69–75.

E. Ketz and R. Kochanek, 'Cash Flow: Assessing a Company's Real Financial Health', *Financial Executive*, July 1982, pp. 34–40.

J.A. Largay and C.P. Stickney, 'Cash Flows, Ratio Analysis and the W.T. Grant Company Bankruptcy', *Financial Analysts Journal*, July-August 1980, pp. 51–4.

G.H. Lawson, *Applications of a Business Theory*, University of Liverpool Press, 1968.

G.H. Lawson, 'Profit Maximisation Via Financial Management', *Management Decision*, Winter 1969, pp. 6–12.

G.H. Lawson, 'Measuring Divisional Performance', *Management Accountant*, May 1971, pp. 147–52.

G.H. Lawson, 'Accounting for Financial Management – Some Tentative Proposals for a New Blueprint', in R. Shone (ed.), *Problems of Investment*, Blackwell, 1971, pp. 36–64.

G.H. Lawson, 'Cash-flow Accounting', *The Accountant*, 28 October 1971, pp. 586–9; 4 November 1971, pp. 620–2.

G.H. Lawson, 'Distributable Profits and Dividends', *Management International Review*, Vol. 12 (2–3), 1971, pp. 113–9.

G.H. Lawson, 'The Rationale for Measuring the Cost of Working Capital', *Working*

Paper Series 15, Manchester Business School 1975.

G.H. Lawson, 'The Rationale of Cash Flow Accounting', in C. van Dam (ed.), *Trends in Managerial and Financial Accounting*, Martinus Nijhoff, 1978, pp. 85–104.

G.H. Lawson, *Company Profitability and the U.K. Stock Market – An Exercise in Cash Flow Accounting*, Manchester Business School, 1978.

G.H. Lawson, 'The Measurement of Corporate Profitability on a Cash Flow Basis', in B.E. Hicks and P. Hunt (eds.), *Cash Flow Accounting*, Laurentian University, 1981, pp. 40–80.

G.H. Lawson and A.W. Stark, 'The Concept of Profit for Fund Raising', *Accounting and Business Research*, Winter 1975, pp. 21–41.

B.A. Rutherford, 'Cash Flow Reporting and Distributional Allocations: A Note', *Journal of Business Finance and Accounting*, Spring 1983, pp. 313–6.

B.A. Rutherford, 'The Interpretation of Cash Flow Reports and the Other Allocation Problem', *Abacus*, June 1982, pp. 40–9.

G.J. Staubus, *A Theory of Accounting for Investors*, University of California Press, 1961, pp. 134–6.

G.J. Staubus, 'Alternative Asset Flow Concepts', *The Accounting Review*, July 1966, pp. 397–412.

A.L. Thomas, 'The Allocation Problem', *Studies in Accounting Research 3*, American Accounting Association, 1969, p. 101 and pp. 108–9.

A.L. Thomas, 'The Allocation Problem: Part Two', *Studies in Accounting Research 9*, American Accounting Association, 1974, pp. 119–22.

A.L. Thomas, 'Matching: Up from Our Black Hole', in R.R. Sterling and A.L. Thomas (eds.), *Accounting for a Simplified Firm*, Scholars Book Co., 1979, pp. 11–33.

A.L. Thomas, 'Cash-Flow Reporting as Allocation-Free Disclosure: A Polemic', in B.E. Hicks and P. Hunt (eds.), *Cash Flow Accounting*, Laurentian University, 1981, pp. 126–32.

D.P. Tweedie, 'Cash Flows and Realizable Values: the Intuitive Concepts? An Empirical Test', *Accounting and Business Research*, Winter 1977, pp. 2–13.

Writings on sale price accounting are numerous, and are not usually described as part of cash flow accounting. A suitable bibliography of sale price accounting is contained in T.A. Lee, *Income and Value Measurement: Theory and Practice*, Van Nostrand Reinhold (UK), 1980.

Workings

CHAPTER 1

(a) £28 + 28 + 28 + 36
(b) £20 + 20 + 25 + 25
(c) £30 + 30
(d) £28 + 36
(e) £80 + 56 − 90
(f) £30 + 30
(g) £80 − 46
(h) £28 + 28
(i) £20 + 20 + 25 + 25

CHAPTER 2

(a) 3 × £75
(b) 3 × £50
(c) 2 × £75
(d) 6 × £50
(e) 4 × £12
(f) 4 × £9
(g) (4 × £12) + (7 × £14)
(h) (4 × £9) + (7 × £11)
(i) (4 × £12) + (7 × £14)
(j) (10 × £9) + (16 × £11)
(k) 7 × £14
(l) 7 × £11
(m) 1/6 × £6,000
(n) £6,000 − 3,500
(o) £900 + 100
(p) 0.7 × £2,000
(q) £400 − 0
(r) £2,000 − 1,400
(s) £6,500 + 2,500
(t) £1,700 − 250
(u) £6,400 − 2,500 + 250

CHAPTER 3

(a) £22,000 − 8,000
(b) £32,000 − 9,000
(c) 4 × £10,000 ; (3 × £10,000) + (1 × £14,000)
(d) 2 × 1/4 × £40,000 ; (3 × 1/4 × £30,000) + (1 × 1/4 × £14,000)
(e) 4 × £10,000 ; (3 × £10,000) + (1 × £14,000)
(f) 2 × 1/5 × £40,000 ; (3 × 1/5 × £30,000) + (1 × 1/5 × £14,000)
(g) £18,200 − 8,000
(h) 4 × £12,500 ; (3 × £15,500) + (1 × £15,500)
(i) 2 × 1/4 × £50,000 ; (3 × 1/4 × £46,500) + (1 × 1/4 × £15,500)
(j) £4,000 + (25,000 − 20,000) ; £13,000 + (23,250 − 18,000)
(k) £18,250 − 9,000
(l) 4 × £4,000 ; (3 × £1,800) + 8,000
(m) 4,000 + (16,000 − 20,000) ; £13,000 + (13,400 − 18,000)
(n) 121/100 × £40,000; (133/100 × £30,000) + (133/121 × £14,000)
(o) 2 × 1/4 × $£_p$48,400; (3 × 1/4 × $£_p$39,900) + (1 × 1/4 × $£_p$15,388)
(p) 121/100 × £10,000; 133/100 × £10,000
(q) For simplicity, and due to lack of detailed information, taken as the balancing figure.
(r) 133/121 × $£_p$18,200
(s) 121/100 × £10,000 ; 133/100 × £10,000
(t) For simplicity, and due to lack of detailed information, taken as the balancing figure.
(u) 133/121 × $£_p$19,000
(v) 121/100 × £10,000 ; 133/100 × £10,000
(w) For simplicity, and due to lack of detailed information, taken as the balancing figure.
(x) 133/121 × $£_p$10,000
(y) Now given, and reconciling to increase in bank balance £12,000 − increase in creditors £1,000 + purchase of vehicle £14,000.
(z) 1/4 × £62,000
(aa) (1/2 × £12,500) − 0
(bb) (4 × £15,500) − (3 × £12,500) − (1 × £14,000)
(cc) (1/2 × 3 × £15,500) − (1/2 × 3 × £12,500)
(dd) Reconciling to profit before depreciation £25,000 + increase in creditors £1,000

CHAPTER 4

(a) £1,000 + 500
(b) £8,000 − 2,000
(c) 1/10 × £1,000
(d) £1,000 − 100
(e) £1,000 + (10,000 − 1,000) − (8,000 − 200) − 1,000 − 1,500
(f) £2,000 − 0
(g) £1,000 − 0
(h) £(200) − (0)
(i) £1,000 − 0
(j) £2,000 + 1,000 − 200 − 300
(k) £10,000 − 1,000

(l) £8,000 – 200
(m) £2,000 + 1,000 – 200 (excluding the overdraft)
(n) 1/10 × £1,200
(o) £1,200 – 120
(p) £7,500 – 6,000
(q) £2,800 – 2,000
(r) £1,200 – 1,000
(s) £2,380 + 1,500 + 800 + 200
(t) £2,380 + 1,500 + 800 + 200
(u) £2,800 + 1,000 – 200 – 300
(v) £7,500 – 6,000
(w) £120 – 100
(x) £1,500 + 20
(y) (£2,800 – 2,000) + (£1,200 – 1,000 – 20)
(z) £1,000 + 1,520 + 980
(aa) £1,000 + 1,520 + 980 + 880
(bb) £1,000 – 700
(cc) £3,800 – 2,000
(dd) £9,000 – 7,800
(ee) £7,500 – 6,000
(ff) £120 – 100
(gg) £2,800 – 2,000
(hh) £1,080 – 900

CHAPTER 5

(a) Required in order to obtain the historic cost of goods sold.
(b) Required in order to obtain a measure of historic cost profit for purposes, say, of taxation.
(c) Balancing figures required to produce the period-end asset data in sale price terms. These figures partly reflect periodic changes in sale price, and partly adjustments to cater for a mixture of historic costs and sale prices.
(d) As per the Statement of Realized Cash Flow.
(e) Assuming that the property could be sold without disrupting the operations of the business.
(f) Assuming the property could be sold without disrupting the operations of the business.
(g) 1978 = £24,000 × 110/100 – £24,000
1979 = £66,000 × 121/110 – £66,000
1980 = £90,000 × 133/121 – £90,000
1981 = £94,000 × 146/133 – £94,000
1982 = £95,000 × 161/146 – £95,000
(All figures taken to the nearest £000).
(h) 1978 = £0 + 2,000
1979 = £2,000 + 7,000
1980 = £9,000 + 9,000
1981 = £18,000 + 9,000
1982 = £27,000 + 10,000
(i) As per Statement of Maintained Realizable Earnings.

CHAPTER 6

(a) As per Statement of Realizable Earnings (1).
(b) As per Statement of Realized Cash Flow.
(c) For example, the 1978 figure can be derived from the CFR worksheet for UV in Chapter 5:

	£
Increase in stock of finished goods (£125,000 – 119,000)	6,000
Increase in work-in-progress (£133,000 – 125,000)	8,000
Increase in debtors (£194,000 – 187,000)	7,000
	21,000
Less: increase in creditors (£133,000 – 124,000)	9,000
Increase in working capital	12,000

These figures are derived from historic cost data, and reflect the double-entry bookkeeping relationship between historic cost profit and operating cash flow. The figures for 1979 to 1982, inclusive, can be derived from equivalent data in Appendices 1-4.

(d) In each case, see Statement of Realizable Earnings (2).
(e) See Statement of Realized Cash Flow.
(f) See Statement of Financial Position and Statement of Change in Financial Position.
(g) £60,000 – 11,000
(h) £63,000 – 18,000
(i) £5,000 – 0
(j) £22,000 – 10,000
(k) £60,000/123,000
(l) £111,000 + 84,000 + 107,000
(m) £16,000/10,000
(n) Credit (days) using total credit purchases was slightly less in each case but did not substantially alter the picture – 37, 49, 47, 53, 49 days, respectively.
(o) Assuming the tax department has priority of repayment over other creditors.
(p) Increase = £40,000 – 11,000 = £29,000
Percentage = £29,000/11,000 × 100
(q) Increase = £264,000 – 194,000 = £70,000
Percentage = £70,000/194,000 × 100
(r) £5,000 – 0
(s) Taking the reasonable assumption of taxation liabilities as a first charge against available cash.
(t) Assumed to be a reasonable deduction from trading results, and equivalent to conventional tax allowances if 100% rates are postulated.
(u) £160 – 120
(v) £40 – 20

CHAPTER 7

(a) £45,000 + 9,000 − 3,000
(b) £23,000 + 9,000 − 3,000
(c) £45,000 + 23,000

(d)

1980–2	*1981–3*	*1982–4*	*1983–5*
1000	1000	1000	1000
4+4+13	4+13+17	13+17+16	17+16+22

(e) 1980–2, 1981–3, 1982–4 and 1983–5 as page 102.
1980–5 = £000 4 + 4 + 13 + 17 + 16 + 22

(f)

1980–2	*1981–3*	*1982–4*	*1983–5*	*1980–5*
£000	£000	£000	£000	£000
0+2+14	2+14+14	14+14+11	14+11+19	0+2+14+14+11+19

(g)

1980–2	*1981–3*	*1982–4*	*1983–5*	*1980–5*
£000	£000	£000	£000	£000
0+0+15	0+15+15	15+15+10	15+10+20	0+0+15+15+10+20

(h)

1980–2	*1981–3*	*1982–4*	*1983–5*	*1980–5*
£000	£000	£000	£000	£000
2+4+8	4+8+10	8+10+10	10+10+14	2+4+8+10+10+14

(i)

1980–2	*1981–3*	*1982–4*	*1983–5*	*1980–5*
£000	£000	£000	£000	£000
2+2+4	2+4+6	4+6+7	6+7+7	2+2+4+6+7+7

	1980–2	*1981–3*	*1982–4*	*1983–5*	*1980–5*
(j)	21/37 × 100	34/64 × 100	46/85 × 100	55/99 × 100	76/136 × 100
(k)	16/37 × 100	30/64 × 100	39/85 × 100	44/99 × 100	60/136 × 100
(l)	15/37 × 100	30/64 × 100	40/85 × 100	45/99 × 100	60/136 × 100
(m)	14/37 × 100	22/64 × 100	28/85 × 100	34/99 × 100	48/136 × 100
(n)	8/37 × 100	12/64 × 100	17/85 × 100	20/99 × 100	28/136 × 100

(o)

1980	*1981*	*1982*	*1983*
£000	£000	£000	£000
$\frac{12+20}{5+10+4+2}$	$\frac{22+37}{7+20+8+4}$	$\frac{27+53}{21+23+10+6}$	$\frac{30+71}{35+26+10+7}$
1984	*1985*		
£000	£000		
$\frac{48+92}{46+43+14+7}$	$\frac{62+115}{65+57+13+8}$		

(p)

1980	*1981*	*1982*	*1983*
£000	£000	£000	£000
$\frac{20}{5+10+4+2}$	$\frac{37}{7+20+8+4}$	$\frac{53}{21+23+10+6}$	$\frac{71}{35+26+10+7}$
1984	*1985*		
£000	£000		
$\frac{92}{46+43+14+7}$	$\frac{115}{65+57+13+8}$		

(q) Taken as the relationship between purchases for the year (cost of sales + closing stock – opening stock) to average stock for the year, and related to a twelve month period:

1980 £000	*1981* £000
$\dfrac{64 + 12 - 10}{\dfrac{10 + 12}{2}} = 6.0\ ;\dfrac{12}{6}$	$\dfrac{99 + 22 - 12}{\dfrac{12 + 22}{2}} = 6.4\ ;\dfrac{12}{6.4}$

1982 £000	*1983* £000
$\dfrac{157 + 27 - 22}{\dfrac{22 + 27}{2}} = 6.6\ ;\dfrac{12}{6.6}$	$\dfrac{181 + 30 - 27}{\dfrac{27 + 30}{2}} = 6.5\ ;\dfrac{12}{6.5}$

1984 £000	*1985* £000
$\dfrac{236 + 48 - 30}{\dfrac{30 + 48}{2}} = 6.5\ ;\dfrac{12}{6.5}$	$\dfrac{329 + 62 - 48}{\dfrac{48 + 62}{2}} = 6.2\ ;\dfrac{12}{6.2}$

(r) Taken as the relationship between sales for the year and average debtors for the year, and related to a twelve month period:

1980 £000	*1981* £000
$\dfrac{84}{\dfrac{12 + 20}{2}} = 5.3\ ;\dfrac{12}{5.3}$	$\dfrac{130}{\dfrac{20 + 37}{2}} = 4.6\ ;\dfrac{12}{4.6}$

1982 £000	*1983* £000
$\dfrac{206}{\dfrac{37 + 53}{2}} = 4.6\ ;\dfrac{12}{4.6}$	$\dfrac{237}{\dfrac{53 + 71}{2}} = 3.8\ ;\dfrac{12}{3.8}$

1984 £000	*1985* £000
$\dfrac{299}{\dfrac{71 + 92}{2}} = 3.7\ ;\dfrac{12}{3.7}$	$\dfrac{410}{\dfrac{92 + 115}{2}} = 4.0\ ;\dfrac{12}{4.0}$

(s) Taken as the relationship between purchases for the year (cost of sales + closing stock – opening stock) and average creditors for the year, and related to a twelve month period:

1980 £000	*1981* £000
$\dfrac{64 + 12 - 10}{\dfrac{9 + 10}{2}} = 6.9\ ;\dfrac{12}{6.9}$	$\dfrac{99 + 22 - 12}{\dfrac{10 + 20}{2}} = 7.3\ ;\dfrac{12}{7.3}$

1982 £000	1983 £000
$\dfrac{157 + 27 + 22}{\dfrac{20 + 23}{2}} = 7.5\ ;\dfrac{12}{7.5}$	$\dfrac{181 + 30 - 27}{\dfrac{23 + 26}{2}} = 7.5\ ;\dfrac{12}{7.5}$

1984 £000	1985 £000
$\dfrac{236 + 48 - 30}{\dfrac{26 + 43}{2}} = 7.4\ ;\dfrac{12}{7.4}$	$\dfrac{329 + 62 - 48}{\dfrac{43 + 57}{2}} = 6.9\ ;\dfrac{12}{6.9}$

(t)

1980 £000	1981 £000	1982 £000	1983 £000	1984 £000	1985 £000
$\frac{4}{2}$	$\frac{8}{4}$	$\frac{13}{6}$	$\frac{14}{7}$	$\frac{11}{7}$	$\frac{19}{8}$

(u)

1980 £000	1981 £000	1982 £000	1983 £000	1984 £000	1985 £000
$\frac{20}{84} \times 100$	$\frac{31}{130} \times 100$	$\frac{49}{206} \times 100$	$\frac{56}{237} \times 100$	$\frac{63}{299} \times 100$	$\frac{81}{410} \times 100$

(v)

1980 £000	1981 £000	1982 £000	1983 £000	1984 £000	1985 £000
$\frac{8}{84} \times 100$	$\frac{16}{130} \times 100$	$\frac{23}{206} \times 100$	$\frac{24}{237} \times 100$	$\frac{25}{299} \times 100$	$\frac{32}{410} \times 100$

(w)

1980 £000	1981 £000	1982 £000
$\dfrac{8}{\frac{60+62}{2}} \times 100$	$\dfrac{16}{\frac{62+85}{2}} \times 100$	$\dfrac{23}{\frac{85+92}{2}} \times 100$

1983 £000	1984 £000	1985 £000
$\dfrac{24}{\frac{92+99}{2}} \times 100$	$\dfrac{25}{\frac{99+123}{2}} \times 100$	$\dfrac{32}{\frac{123+134}{2}} \times 100$

(x)

1980 £000	1981 £000	1982 £000	1983 £000	1984 £000	1985 £000	Total £000
13	21	31	35	38	45	183

(y)

1980 £000	1981 £000	1982 £000	1983 £000	1984 £000	1985 £000	Total £000
4	4	13	17	16	22	76

(z)

	1980 £000	1981 £000	1982 £000	1983 £000	1984 £000	1985 £000	Total £000
Increase in:							
stock	2	10	5	3	18	14	52
debtors	8	17	16	18	21	23	103
(creditors)	(1)	(10)	(3)	(3)	(17)	(14)	(48)
	9	17	18	18	22	23	107

(aa) £76,000 + 60,000

(bb)

1980 £000	1981 £000	1982 £000	1983 £000	1984 £000	1985 £000	Total £000
5	5	8	11	13	13	55

(cc)

1980 £000	1981 £000	1982 £000	1983 £000	1984 £000	1985 £000	Total £000
—	—	15	15	10	20	60

(dd)

1980 £000	1981 £000	1982 £000	1983 £000	1984 £000	1985 £000	Total £000
4	8	10	10	14	13	59

(ee)

1980 £000	1981 £000	1982 £000	1983 £000	1984 £000	1985 £000	Total £000
2	4	6	7	7	8	34

(ff)

1980 £000	1981 £000	1982 £000	1983 £000	1984 £000	1985 £000	Total £000
2	4	8	10	10	14	48

(gg)

1980 £000	1981 £000	1982 £000	1983 £000	1984 £000	1985 £000	Total £000
2	2	4	6	7	7	28

CHAPTER 8

(a)

1980	*1981*	*1982*	*1983*
4/11 × 100	4/27 × 100	13/29 × 100	17/32 × 100
1984	*1985*		
16/39 × 100	22/36 × 100		

(b)

1980	*1981*	*1982*	*1983*
7/11 × 100	23/27 × 100	16/29 × 100	15/32 × 100
1984	*1985*		
23/39 × 100	14/36 × 100		

(c) Total assets have been taken as the base line for these calculations.

(d)

1979	*1980*	*1981*	*1982*
18/81 × 100	21/89 × 100	39/122 × 100	60/156 × 100
1983	*1984*	*1985*	
78/189 × 100	110/239 × 100	143/287 × 100	

(e)

1979	*1980*	*1981*	*1982*
63/81 × 100	68/89 × 100	83/122 × 100	96/156 × 100
1983	*1984*	*1985*	
111/189 × 100	129/239 × 100	144/287 × 100	

(f) £18,000 in 1979; £143,000 in 1985

(g) £63,000 in 1979; £144,000 in 1985

(h)

1979	*1980*	*1981*	*1982*	*1983*	*1984*	*1985*
£000	£000	£000	£000	£000	£000	£000
5/68	5/73	7/90	21/117	35/146	46/175	65/209

(and then each multiplied by 100)

(i) In each year, total assets divided by the bank overdraft.

(j)

1980	*1981*	*1982*
£000	£000	£000
$\frac{81 + 89}{2}$	$\frac{89 + 122}{2}$	$\frac{122 + 156}{2}$
1983	*1984*	*1985*
£000	£000	£000
$\frac{156 + 189}{2}$	$\frac{189 + 239}{2}$	$\frac{239 + 287}{2}$

(k)

1980	*1981*	*1982*
£000	£000	£000
5/85 × 100	5/106 × 100	14/139 × 100
1983	*1984*	*1985*
£000	£000	£000
20/173 × 100	22/214 × 100	29/263 × 100

(l)

1980	*1981*	*1982*
£000	£000	£000
12/85 × 100	28/106 × 100	30/139 × 100
1983	*1984*	*1985*
£000	£000	£000
35/173 × 100	45/214 × 100	43/263 × 100

(m)

1980	*1981*	*1982*
£000	£000	£000
$\frac{63 + 68}{2}$	$\frac{68 + 83}{2}$	$\frac{83 + 96}{2}$
1983	*1984*	*1985*
£000	£000	£000
$\frac{96 + 111}{2}$	$\frac{111 + 129}{2}$	$\frac{129 + 144}{2}$

(n)

1980	*1981*	*1982*
£000	£000	£000
4/66 × 100	4/76 × 100	13/90 × 100
1983	*1984*	*1985*
£000	£000	£000
17/104 × 100	16/120 × 100	22/137 × 100

(o)

1980	*1981*	*1982*
£000	£000	£000
11/66 × 100	27/76 × 100	29/90 × 100
1983	*1984*	*1985*
£000	£000	£000
32/104 × 100	39/120 × 100	36/137 × 100

(p)	*1980*	*1981*	*1982*
	£000	£000	£000
	89/21	122/39	156/60
	1983	*1984*	*1985*
	£000	£000	£000
	189/78	239/110	287/143
(q)	*1980*	*1981*	*1982*
	£000	£000	£000
	35/16	64/32	86/39
	1983	*1984*	*1985*
	£000	£000	£000
	107/43	150/64	189/78

Index